What Every Teacher Should Know About Transition and IDEA 2004

Carol A. Kochhar-Bryant
The George Washington University

with

Stan Shaw and Margo Izzo

Upper Saddle River, New Jersey
Columbus, Ohio

Printed in the United States of America

10 9 8 7 6 5 4 3 2 1   11 10 09 08

Merrill
is an imprint of

ISBN-10:   0-13-715586-7
ISBN-13:   978-0-13-715587-6

www.pearsonhighered.com

Contents

Chapter 1

Transition Services for Youths: New Requirements in IDEA 2004 and NCLB

*Transition is not just a fad. It is not a program or a project that has a
beginning and an end. It is a vision and a framework for assisting
youths to define their futures, take responsibility, and make continuous
progress toward their long-range life goals.*

What Is the Purpose of This Book?

The purpose of this book is to introduce the concept and processes of
transition services for youths with disabilities that are required under the
Individuals with Disabilities Education Act of 2004 (IDEA 2004, P.L.
108-476) and the No Child Left Behind Act of 2001 (NCLB, P.L.107-
110). The book addresses several questions:

- Why is transition important for youths and who benefits?
- What provisions in IDEA 2004 and NCLB 2001 promote transition
  services?
- What changes for youths as they move from secondary to postschool
  environments?
- How are transition plans created and what is the role of the IEP
  team?
- How are transition and standards-based education connected?
- What is the new Summary of Performance under IDEA 2004?

The book describes effective practices for transition that special and
general education teachers, transition coordinators, school and guidance
counselors, administrators, and others can use within today's standards-
based educational settings. The book challenges the reader to look
beyond the statutory requirements to consider the broader intent of the
laws. For all students, decisions about postsecondary choices are individual. For youths with disabilities these decisions can be especially complex
and require individualized advanced planning processes. Transition,
therefore, must be viewed as a flexible, comprehensive, and coordinated
planning process for the individual student, offering options and choices
that are aimed at well-defined postsecondary goals. We hope that this

work provides useful, practical information and tools for professionals, consumer advocates, students, and families seeking to improve upon current transition practices.

Appendix 1 compares IDEA 1997 and IDEA 2004 provisions related to transition services, and Appendix 2 presents transition-related provisions under NCLB 2001. These laws complement each other to strengthen transition services for all youths, particularly those with disabilities and those at risk as they enter postsecondary education, employment, and adult responsibilities.

The last section provides an introduction to the Summary of Performance (SOP), which is required by IDEA 2004 for all youths with Individualized Education Programs (IEP) who are in their final year before graduation. A template is presented, designed by a national committee of professionals who represent secondary education, post-secondary education, parents, consumer advocates, and professional associations.

This book is written for general and special education teachers, related services personnel, administrators, paraprofessionals and other school-based professionals concerned with preparing youths for transition to the adult world. The content may also be useful for teacher-leaders and administrators who wish to design professional development training for new and veteran personnel.

Chapter 2

Why Is Transition Important for Youths and Who Benefits?

Summary of Conditions for Youths

Research has documented continuing gaps between young people with disabilities and their nondisabled peers with regard to education, transition, economic, and independent living outcomes. Below is a summary of the conditions for youths with disabilities in the United States as reflected in several major studies and reports on youths' outcomes over the past decade.

1. Twenty-two percent (22%) of Americans with disabilities fail to complete high school, compared to 9 percent of those without disabilities. Compared with their nondisabled peers, they are more likely to be unemployed, live with parents and be socially isolated (Kortering & Braziel, 2000; National Organization on Disability, 2003).

2. People with disabilities, ages 18–64, are less likely to be employed (32% either full-time or part-time) than people without disabilities (81%). This gap of 49 percentage points is the largest of all the gaps and may help to explain the persistence of other gaps in income, employment, and health care (National Organization on Disability, 2003).

3. Students with disabilities are less likely to have taken advanced mathematics and English courses in high school and more likely to have taken remedial courses. They tend to have a lower high school grade point average and lower scores on the Scholastic Aptitude Test (SAT) than students without disabilities (National Center on Education Statistics, NCES, 1999).

4. Students with disabilities who enroll in postsecondary institutions are less likely to complete a bachelors degree (16% versus 27% respectively) and 11 percent of college graduates with disabilities are unemployed, compared to 4 percent of those without disabilities (NCES, 1999).

5. Youths who attend college often experience negative self-concept, poor socialization skills, stress and anxiety, and professors reluctant to help (National Center for the Study of Postsecondary Educational Supports, 2002, p. 11; Sitlington & Clark, 2006).

3

6. Only 28.4 percent of Americans with disabilities have access to the Internet at home or work, compared to 56.7 percent of those without disabilities. Almost 60 percent of Americans with disabilities have never even used a personal computer, compared to less than 25 percent of Americans without disabilities (Kaye, 2000; National Organization on Disability, 2000).
7. Studies of transition plans for students show that they do not reflect the requirements of IDEA 1997 or 2004, and there are systematic problems throughout the states (Sitlington & Clark, 2006; Storms, O'Leary, & Williams, 2000). Youths with disabilities are also less likely to participate in after-school activities, enrichment programs, and community-based youth programs.
8. An increasing number of youths apply for Supplemental Security Income (SSI) or Social Security Disability Income (SSDI) each year, despite significant federal, state, and local investments in special education. About 60,000 between ages 18–24 come on the rolls annually and less than 1 percent ever leave (Berry & Jones, 2000; Social Security Administration Annual Statistics, 2001).

These conditions highlight the need for a *greater national commitment to coordinated transition planning and support* for youths.

Youth Participation in the Work Force after High School

Despite decades of federal and state initiatives to improve employment outcomes for youths with disabilities, there has not been a substantial increase in the numbers of persons with disabilities participating in the workforce (Blanck, 2000; Gaylord, 2004) unless they complete a college degree. Employment outcomes continue to reflect the widest gulf between youths with disabilities and the general population. According to the Census Bureau (McNeil, 2000), only three in ten working-age people with disabilities are employed full-time, compared to eight in ten people in the rest of the population. Working-age people with disabilities are no more likely to be employed today than they were a decade ago, even though almost 75 percent who are not working say they would prefer to be working (National Council on Disability, 2000). Three to five years after high school only about half (50%) of young people with disabilities were employed, compared to 69 percent of their peers (Fabian, Lent, & Willis, 1998; McNeil, 2000; Wagner et al., 2005). Students with disabilities need greater assistance to prepare to enter employment upon graduation from high school.

4

Preparing Youths for Postsecondary Education

Recent studies show that youths with disabilities are not adequately prepared to meet the entrance requirements and academic rigor of postsecondary institutions (Shaw, 2005). Students with disabilities are less likely than their peers without disabilities to complete a full secondary school academic curriculum, especially in math and science curriculum areas. Furthermore, they are often not encouraged in high school to extend their education beyond secondary school. Youths with disabilities drop out of high school at twice the rate of their peers without disabilities (National Organization on Disability, 2003); the dropout rate for all disabilities is currently 41.1 percent, up from 45.1 percent in 1993–2003 (U.S. Department of Education, 2003). For students with emotional and behavioral disabilities, the rate is 65.1 percent (U.S. Department of Education, 2003).

Recent research also shows that secondary students with disabilities generally have minimal involvement in their Individualized Education Program (IEP) meetings (Abery & Stancliffe, 1996; National Council on Disability, 2003; Storms, O'Leary, & Williams, 2000). As a result, they are disengaged from postsecondary transition planning and unprepared to self-advocate for their needs once they leave high school. When ranked according to how qualified they were for college admission, students with disabilities were much less likely to be even minimally qualified, based on an index score of grades, class rank, National Education Longitudinal Study (NELS) composite test scores, and SAT/ACT scores (NCES, 1999; Wagner et al., 2005).

The supports that postsecondary institutions provide to students with disabilities are typically different than those offered by their high schools, making the transition more difficult. They may not have the resources to ensure that all accommodations and services are provided to all students who need them (National Center for Secondary Education and Transition, 2004). Greater efforts are needed to keep youths engaged in secondary education and in planning for their future.

Youth Participation and Outcomes of Postsecondary Education

Young adults with disabilities who complete a college degree are *more likely to become employed and earn higher wages* than non-college completers without disabilities. However, young people with disabilities lag behind their peers without disabilities on every measure of long-range educational success: college graduation rates, long-term employment after college, participation in advanced education, and independent living (National Center for Secondary Education and Transition, 2004; Wagner et al., 2005). In comparison with their non-disabled peers, individuals with disabilities are less than half as likely to obtain a postsecondary degree, and therefore to achieve similar incomes (National Organization on Disability, 2003; Wagner et al., 2005). Greater commitment from higher education is needed to recruit and retain students with disabilities.

Continuing Need for Individualized Transition Planning

The transition service planning for young people with disabilities requires an individualized approach based on the unique needs of the student. Research studies reveal, however, that such "customized" services continue to be elusive:

- Only one-third of young people with disabilities who need job training actually receive it.
- Only one-fourth of young people who need life skills training, tutoring, interpreting, or personal counseling services receive them.
- Contacts with vocational rehabilitation agencies, postsecondary institutions, job placement programs, employers, social service and mental health agencies are substantially less frequent for youths with serious emotional disabilities. Within three to five years after exiting school, more than half of these youths are arrested at least once (National Council on Disability, 2003).
- Teachers often view the completion of the Transition Component of the IEP as "paperwork," not as a document intended to reflect a transition team's postschool plan and vision for a student (Cameto, Marder, Wagner, & Cardoso, 2003; Destafano, Heck, Hazasi, & Furney, 1999; National Council on Disability, 2003; Storms, O'Leary, & Williams, 2000; Thompson, Fulk, & Piercy, 2000).

The absence of positive secondary education and transition outcomes points to the need to move beyond the technical requirements of IDEA and view transition planning as a thoughtful, unified set of goals and plans that will lead to an individualized course of action for each student (Thompson, Fulk, & Piercy, 2000). Systematic linkages are needed among schools, community agencies, the business community, and higher education to extend the benefits of transition services.

Who Benefits from Transition Services?

Research on youth outcomes has attested to the benefits of transition services for students with disabilities. Such development can be observed in many local school districts in which there are strong interagency

agreements between the schools and community agencies that share responsibility for transition services to youths with disabilities. The benefits of transition services for many stakeholders are summarized below.

Benefits to Students

When students receive comprehensive transition services and
participate in transition planning, their preparation for postsecondary
education and employment improves. Research has demonstrated a
relationship between students' involvement in their own individualized
educational planning and transition goal setting and improved postsecondary outcomes (Martin, 2002; Martin, Huber, Marshall & Depry,
2001). Such involvement in personal goal setting and exercise of decision
making is referred to as *self-determination,* or *self-advocacy.* Students
experience higher self-esteem and personal success as a result of
interaction with nondisabled peers and others in the community. A wider
"circle of support" and social support system, which includes nondisabled classmates, is correlated with improved social skills development, positive behaviors, and improved learning (Bremer et al., 2003).
Students also experience improved learning from working in community-
based learning teams and increased enjoyment of the social interaction in
community-based employment and training settings. Overall, youths
experience a greater adjustment to adult roles as a result of their participation in a supportive transition planning process.

Benefits to Parents and Guardians

The transition planning process links parents with teachers, counselors, and related services personnel, includes parents in the school-to-
work transition planning process, and prepares professionals to help
parents strengthen personal decision making, goal setting, and self-
advocacy in their children.

Two- and Four-Year Colleges and Technical Schools

Colleges and universities benefit from students' preparation for
transition to postsecondary education. When students understand their
strengths and disabilities and the change in their status as they leave
secondary education, they become more realistic in their expectations
and can better self-advocate for reasonable accommodations in the
postsecondary setting. When they are better prepared to make decisions
about their future, they are more likely to enroll in and complete
advanced education and to enter and sustain employment (Benz,
Lindstrom, & Yovonoff, 2000; General Accounting Office, 2003;
Wehmeyer, 2003).

7

Benefits to Community Agencies

Systematic transition services promote collaboration among related service agencies and personnel to better support youths with disabilities who are participating in general secondary education or career-vocational education classes. Interagency coordination for transition stimulates resource sharing among schools and community service agencies and promotes systematic assessment of services and evaluation (Dunst & Bruder, 2002; Research and Training Center on Service Coordination, 2001).

Benefits to Businesses and the Community at Large

Transition services promote innovative linkages between schools and the business community to provide career-related work experiences in real-world work settings. Transition programs transform the role of the business and community agency partners from that of donors/philanthropists to active partners in school restructuring. Such partnerships help connect career-vocational education programs with the expectations and environments of today's industries.

Benefits to At-Risk Youths

Individualized transition programs provide strategies to motivate students with disabilities and those at risk of school dropout to remain in school to complete their degrees. Transition programs often employ creative and integrated academic-vocational-technical curricula, combined with alternative student performance assessments such as exhibitions, demonstrations, and individualized work projects. Flexibility in curriculum and assessment can keep students engaged and motivated to stay in school.

Benefits to the Nation

Transition services help expand the pool of qualified and skilled workers, which ultimately reduces young adults' dependence on the family or public support. Successful transition leads to increased participation of youths and young adults with disabilities in civic activities and the political process. National investment in youth transition demonstrates to the nation and the world a national commitment to the welfare, self-determination, and full participation of all residents in communities across the United States.

Chapter 3

Is Transition a New Idea?

A Thumbnail History

Over the past 20 years, major transformations have occurred in educational, social, political, and economic arenas that continue to impact the education and development of youths with disabilities and the institutions that support them. Youths with disabilities are now typically educated with their nondisabled peers and antidiscrimination laws have improved access to postsecondary education and employment in a variety of occupations. A greater national investment is being made to assist all individuals to access education and employment preparation programs and increase social and economic independence. Interest in career development and transition is greater than it has ever been in the past, both in the United States and in other nations (Gordon, 1999). Successful transition from secondary education is becoming recognized as a chief indicator of the effectiveness of our educational system for preparing young adults for employment, postsecondary education, and adult independence.

While career development for children, youths, and adults of all exceptionalities has been evolving since the turn of the century, the concept of high school *transition* emerged in the 1950s. More recently, educators and policy makers are recognizing the important role of career and vocational development and high school diploma options in the context of adolescent development. Researchers are interested in the range of interventions believed to be positively associated with improved graduation rates and transition of youths with disabilities from school to employment and adult life roles.

Societal interest in career awareness, career choice, graduation pathways, and adjustment to adult roles has emerged as a new subfield within education. Preparation for transition from school to adult life involves changes in the self-concept, motivation, and development of the individual and is a fragile passage for the adolescent seeking to make difficult life choices (German, Martin, Marshall, & Sale, 2000; Michaels, 1994). This passage is even more delicate for youths with disabilities who need additional support and preparation to make the journey. For professionals seeking to help students on this journey, the process involves forming linkages among education and other human service agencies, including employment and training, adult services, and rehabilitation.

Career Education Becomes a National Priority and Includes Disadvantaged Populations. During the 1970s and 1980s, several education and labor policies were focused on education and training resources to provide extra help to all youths, particularly those special populations who faced severe disadvantages in schools and the workplace. Special populations included those with disabilities, those with limited English proficiency, the economically disadvantaged, teen parents, and those in correctional settings. In the past 25 years, landmark legislation has promoted state and local policies and practices that have helped students with disabilities gain access to appropriate academic, career preparation, transition, and job placement services. Through the 1960s and 1970s, many employment training policies were aimed at easing the transition for all youths and included the 1965 Manpower Development and Training Act (MDTA) in the 1960s, the 1973 Comprehensive Employment and Training Act (CETA), the 1977 Youth Employment Demonstration Act, and the Job Training Partnership Act in the 1980s.

The career education movement in the United States gained additional momentum in the 1960s when it became a high priority of the then U.S. Office of Education's Bureau of Adult, Vocational and Technical Education (Halpern, 1985, 1999). In 1963 the Vocational Education Act (P.L. 88-210) was passed to maintain, extend, and improve upon existing programs of vocational education, and to assist persons who have academic, socioeconomic, or other disadvantages that prevent them from succeeding in regular vocational education (Gordon, 1999). In 1971, career education was proclaimed as a major educational reform by the U.S. Commissioner of Education, Sidney Marland, Jr. Marland believed that the high dropout rate in the United States was due in part to the failure of the educational system to provide students with a "relevant" education that was aligned with their future goals and potentials (Kokaska & Brolin, 1985). Students with disabilities were not included in the initiative originally, but in 1977 the Career Education Implementation Incentive Act (P.L. 95-207) was passed to help states infuse career education into school curricula. Students with disabilities were included as a target population (Michaels, 1994). In 1984, the Vocational Education Act (P.L. 98-524) was passed and named for House Representative Carl D. Perkins, a civil rights supporter who introduced the bill that still bears his name.

Career development under the Perkins Act, and transition services defined in IDEA, have remained enduring concepts and instruments in federal policy over the past half-century to improve secondary education and postsecondary outcomes for youths with disabilities (NCSET, 2002).

Career Education Expanded to Include Youths with Disabilities. During the 1970s, federal involvement in youth development was primarily characterized by an ad-hoc and additive approach to policy making in which special population groups that had been left out were added to existing programs. Educators cautioned policy makers that students with disabilities continued to experience limited access to educational and employment programs. For example, before 1976 vocational education law did not address the participation of youths with disabilities. Many youth advocates view this era of policy making as aimed at leveling the playing field and providing leverage to state and local educational and human service agencies to build their own foundations for *equity* (i.e., improving the general welfare of individuals) and *productivity* (i.e., enhancing the general welfare of communities) (Horne & Morris, 1999).

The 1983 Amendments to the Education of the Handicapped Act (P.L. 98-199), encouraged states and local school districts to voluntarily develop transition supports and services for youths with disabilities. By the end of the 1980s, all 50 states and territories had some form of mandate (laws or state administrative requirements) for school systems to develop school-to-work or school-to-careers services in coordination with other community agencies. After the 1983 Amendments to the Education of the Handicapped Act (P.L. 98-199), most states and local school districts voluntarily developed transition supports and services for youths with disabilities (Halloran & Simon, 1995; Johnson & Rusch, 1993; U.S. Office of Special Education, 1994; Ward & Halloran, 1993).

Defining Transition: An Evolving Idea

Over the past 50 years, many definitions of transition can be found in the literature. Most of them generally refer to a continuing process of movement toward independent adulthood. A seminal publication by Hill in 1969 focused on transition from school to work and reported a study of the changing perceptions of work of 162 children and youths from ages 7 through 18. Hill found that older youths placed more emphasis on the social values of work, that the prospects of transition to the adult world produced anxiety in the individuals, and that youths found it difficult to connect the world of school with the world of work. In 1976, Scharff and Hill described the transition process as a critical stage in life in which an individual brings together his or her internal resources and those gained from adults at school and home to make the first major independent choice that has lasting implications for the future. Young people were required to cope with the personal turbulence inseparable from adolescence, while at the same time experiencing an abrupt change in their institutional environment (p. 68). This collision between the "personal turbulence" of adolescence and the institutional demands on youths presents many barriers to successful transition for all youths, but particularly those with disabilities.

11

1975–1977: Transition Defined as a
Responsibility of the Schools

In 1975, the Education for All Handicapped Children Act (P.L. 94-142) established and reaffirmed the responsibility of the schools to provide appropriate programs of education and training for students with disabilities. Since then, special education and general educational reform laws have promoted and supported the inclusion of students with disabilities with their nondisabled peers in general education classes and extracurricular activities.

In 1977, the former U.S. Department of Health, Education and Welfare (HEW) published a report on federal policy on education and work that examined barriers to the transition of youths to employment and postsecondary education. Successful transition activities were determined to be the responsibility of the schools and included:

a. Providing students with information about the nature and requirements of different occupations, employment prospects, and educational and experience requirements for career entry and advancement;
b. Providing students with information about their own abilities and aptitudes;
c. Providing early socialization of young people into occupational roles;
d. Ensuring that occupational competencies learned in school qualify them for continued education or to entry and advancement through various occupations;
e. Providing job seeking skills and assistance in finding work; and,
f. Strengthening students' work habits and basic skills required for entry-level employment and preparation for advancement in careers (Berman, McLaughlin, Bass-Golod, Pauley, & Zellman, 1977; U.S. Department of Health, Education and Welfare, 1977).

That same year, the Youth Employment and Demonstration Projects Act of 1977 (P.L. 95-93) established a youth employment training program that included—among other activities—promoting education-to-work transition, literacy training and bilingual training, and attainment of certificates of high school equivalency.

1983: Transition Services Are Authorized
under Special Education Law

The definition of the transition process and transition services (which emerged from career education definitions of the 1970s) represented a major policy initiative for special education during the 1970s and 1980s. The difficulties that youths were having as they exited from high schools were brought to the attention of lawmakers by parents, educators, and the research community. In 1983, an amendment to the special education law (P.L. 98-199) was passed that defined "transition services" and authorized a voluntary and discretionary program with funds for which states could compete.

Madeleine Will, then director of the Office of Special Education and Rehabilitative Services of the U.S. Department of Education, defined transition as an *outcome-oriented process* encompassing a broad array of services and experiences that lead to employment, and which are designed to be a bridge from secondary school to employment. Services to assist youths to make a successful transition into employment were divided into three categories: no special services, time-limited services, and ongoing services (Will, 1985). Will's model focused attention on the *shared responsibility* of school and community service agencies (e.g., vocational rehabilitation, mental health services, public health, independent living centers) for improving outcomes for youths as they exit secondary education for employment and adult life. This definition has been modified and greatly expanded since 1983, adding new services and expected outcomes for youths.

1980s: Transition Definition Expands beyond the Employment Domain

Researchers argued that the definition of transition should not be confined solely to the employment outcome or goal, but should be expanded to include other life domains. For example, Halpern (1985) expanded upon Will's definition to include community living and social and interpersonal domains (Halpern, 1985). Halpern's definition was further extended by Wehman, Kregel, Barcus, and Schalock (1986) and redefined as an extended process of planning for the adult life of persons with disabilities and included the domains of employment, independent living, and recreation. Wehman et al. (1986) viewed transition as beginning in the early secondary school years, and involving students, families, school-linked agencies, employers, and other organizations. Wehman et al. recognized the importance of a student's informal networks and home environment upon the success of transition services.

Similarly, Bates, Suter, and Poelvoorde (1986) defined transition as a "dynamic process" involving a partnership of consumers, school-age services, postschool services, and local communities that results in maximum levels of employment, independent living, integration, and community participation. Halpern later augmented his earlier definition, adding "four pillars" for secondary education and transition curriculum: academic skills, vocational skills, social skills, and independent living skills (Halpern, 1993). Figure 3.1 illustrates the evolving development of transition definitions through the 1980s.

Polloway, Patton, Smith, and Roderique (1991) added another dimension, referring to transitions as both *vertical and horizontal.* Vertical transitions are life span developmental transitions associated with major life events such as beginning school, leaving school, and growing older (p. 3). Horizontal transitions refer to movement from one situation or setting to another, such as the movement from a separate setting to a less restrictive, more inclusive setting. These broader conceptions of the transition outcomes helped shape transition policy in the United States and were reflected in both the 1990 and 1997 amendments to IDEA (Greene & Kochhar-Bryant, 2003).

1994: The Council for Exceptional Children Defines Transition

Over a decade ago, the Council for Exceptional Children, Division on Career Development and Transition (DCDT) developed a definition of transition that reflected recent advances in transition practices. The DCDT definition combined the concepts of continuous career develop-

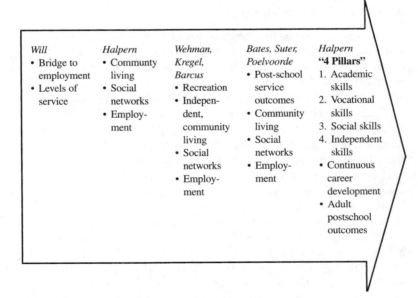

FIGURE 3.1   Transition Evolves through the 1980s

Source: Kochhar-Bryant, C., & Bassett, D. (2003). *Aligning Transition and Standards-Based Education.* Columbus, OH: Merrill/Prentice Hall.

ment from early schooling through high school, recognized the multiple life domains that are encompassed by the term, and emphasized the central role of the individual in the planning process. The DCDT definition is as follows:

> Transition refers to a change in status from behaving primarily as a student to assuming emergent adult roles in the community. These roles include employment, participating in postsecondary education, maintaining a home, becoming appropriately involved in the community and experiencing satisfactory personal and social relationships. The process of enhancing transition involves the participation and coordination of school programs, adult agency services, and natural supports within the community. The foundations for transition should be laid during the elementary and middle school years, guided by the broad concept of career development. Transition planning should begin no later than age 14, and students should be encouraged to the full extent of their capabilities, to assume a maximum amount of responsibility for such planning. (Halpern, 1994, p. 117)

In 1996, Patton and Blalock further advanced the idea that transition involves many domains that are interrelated, including the following:

- postsecondary education
- communication
- relationships/social skills
- self-determination/self-advocacy
- career-vocational training
- employment
- community participation
- independent living
- leisure/recreation
- lifelong learning
- personal management
- vocational evaluation
- transportation/mobility
- advocacy and legal
- daily living
- financial/income/money management
- health

Effective transition programs cannot rely on the efforts of the school system alone, but require partnerships with school-linked agencies and postsecondary institutions (Johnson, Sharpe, & Stodden, 2000; National Council on Disability, 2003; Storms, Williams, & O'Leary, 2000). In recognition of the persistent need to improve transition outcomes for youths, the 1997 Amendments to IDEA modified the definition of transition to emphasize the need for a shared role between school and community agencies.

Secondary Education Reforms and Transition

In the 1990s, partly in reaction to public concerns about the eroding quality of education and weakening economic competitiveness in the United States, policy makers turned their attention to improving student academic achievement. Standards-based reforms have taken center stage in the educational improvement arena. Policy initiatives reflect the widespread belief that improving education depends on the creation of national standards that define what every student should know and be able to do (Center on Education Policy, 2003). The standards-based reform movement has shifted the attention of educators from work and career preparation to academic performance outcomes.

In the 1990s, five additional factors accelerated the implementation of transition services: (1) the passage of the Americans with Disabilities Act (ADA; P.L. 101-336), which sanctioned workplace discrimination against individuals with disabilities; (2) the need for a larger supply of workers in the economy; (3) the recognition of the relationship between transition services and the achievement of postsecondary success for all youths; (4) federal initiatives to promote the development of state transition services; and (5) provisions in the Rehabilitation Act that promote coordination with secondary schools to improve transition services. Although the ad hoc nature of policy making across many government agencies has contributed to an uncoordinated patchwork of youth programs and initiatives, efforts to develop and expand transition practices have endured.

Leaders in education and job training are demanding a systematic redesign of secondary education and transition service delivery for all youths, particularly those with disabilities (Education Policy Reform Research Institute, 2004; Jorgenson, 1998; Patton & Trainor, 2003). Reformers are promoting comprehensive and flexible youth development. Such approaches integrate academic development, social-psychological development, career development, and preparation for work and broader life roles.

For students with the postsecondary goal of employment, flexible curriculum blends both school-based and community-based approaches, particularly during the transition years, grades 9–12, and, if needed, through age 21. During these years, students should be supported to focus on their career goals and much of their learning should occur in the community through work-study or work-based mentorship arrangements. The transition component of the IEP should focus on supports students need to move away from home, establish a social life, become a lifelong learner, and work a part- or full-time job (Jorgenson, 1998, p. 219; Leconte, 2006).

Chapter 4

What Changes in the Laws Affect Transition? IDEA 1997 and 2004, NCLB, and the Rehabilitation Act

How Did IDEA Change from 1997 to 2004?

On December 3, 2004, IDEA 2004 (P.L. 108-446) was signed into law and made several important changes in transition related provisions. It was effective July 1, 2005. Appendix 1 compares language in IDEA 1997 and IDEA 2004 related to transition services for youths. Appendix 2, discussed later, describes important provisions in the No Child Left Behind Act of 2001 (P.L. 107-110) that support transition for all youths, particularly those who are disadvantaged and at risk for failure in the public schools. The following section summarizes the broad changes in transition requirements of IDEA from 1997 to 2004.

Change 1: Initiation of Transition Services Is Moved from Age 14 to 16

The 1990 IDEA required that transition services begin for students at age 16. However, the IDEA of 1997 moved the date of initiation of transition services to age 14 (or younger, if determined appropriate by the IEP team), to be updated annually. The 2004 IDEA shifts the age at which transition services are initiated *from 14 back to age 16* (or younger if determined appropriate by the IEP team).

There were good reasons for Congress's decision to begin the transition process at age 14. Waiting until age 16 was too late for many students to plan an academic or vocational course of study and to provide the needed transition services consistent with the student's postsecondary goals. Research had also shown that when the student is actively involved in the IEP team and in planning their educational program, then he or she is more likely to view school as relevant and is more invested in staying in school (O'Leary & Collision, 2002).

The age 14 provision was also designed to assist youths in their transition from middle to high school, a crucial year of development and adjustment for all youths. As a result, postsecondary outcomes have improved for some students in school districts that provide early planning (Benz, 2000; New York State Department of Education, 2005;

Virginia Department of Education, 2004; Wehmeyer, 2003). Congress explained its decision about the 1997 shift to age 14:

> The purpose of this requirement is to focus attention on how the child's educational program can be planned to help the child make a successful transition to his or her goals for life after secondary school. This provision is designed to augment, and not replace, the separate transition services requirement, under which children with disabilities beginning no later than age sixteen receive transition services, including instruction, community experiences, the development of employment and other post-school objectives, and, when appropriate, independent living skills and functional vocational evaluation (U.S. Congress, 1997).

Whether students choose employment or postsecondary education, they will have to direct their own lives and navigate among a spectrum of community-based service providers and federal, state, and local programs. For many youths this is an overwhelming challenge for which they must be prepared long in advance. The process, therefore, must begin earlier than the final year of high school (before 16) to provide enough time to:

1. Prepare the student to be actively engaged in decision making and the IEP process during high school;
2. Develop a course of study and related transition services that are aligned with the postsecondary goal;
3. Conduct assessments needed to determine appropriate postsecondary goals, transition services, and supports;
4. Prepare the student for self-determination and self-advocacy in the postsecondary setting; and
5. Prepare the youth for adult life in a variety of domains including academic, social, career-vocational, and independent living.

Recognizing the central importance of advanced planning for successful transition, many state and local educational agencies are continuing the practice of beginning comprehensive transition planning at age 14, as was promoted under IDEA 1997 (Glack, 2005). Many are also integrating transition planning into the standards-based framework for students who are in general education classes.

Research has shown a need for early and ongoing transition planning as a means to reduce student alienation, improve attendance, and prevent school dropout (Flexer, Simmons, Luft, & Baer, 2001; Furney & Salembrier, 2000; Martin, Huber, Marshall, & Depry, 2001; Storms, O'Leary, & Williams, 2000). Youths with disabilities are at greatest risk between the ages of 15–18. Poor outcomes for youths with disabilities underscore the need for an early support system and longer range planning, which are crucial for adolescent development and support. According to Hehir, former director of the U.S. Office of Special

Education Programs (1999), high school is a "make-or-break time" for students with disabilities and for too many it is a break time—that's why comprehensive transition planning should begin no later than age 14.

An early support system that includes parents, general and special educators, and related service professionals can strengthen transition planning for middle school students by establishing ways for students to become more involved during the IEP process. Students who are engaged in self-determination activities early in secondary school have also been shown to take greater responsibility for their lives after school (Levine, Marder, & Wagner, 2004). Four of the most fundamental skills or knowledge that students can generalize in a variety of adult situations include the following:

- The ability to assess themselves, including their skills and abilities, and needs associated with their disability;
- Awareness of the accommodations they need;
- Knowledge of their civil rights to these accommodations through legislation such as the IDEA, the Americans with Disabilities Act (ADA), and Section 504 of the Rehabilitation Act of 1973; and,
- The self-advocacy skills necessary to request reasonable accommodations in the workplace, educational institutions, and community settings.

These skills can provide students with a strong base for participating in the development of IEP goals, developing transition plans, and for managing the many aspects of adult life that will become important after high school (Eisenman & Chamberlin, 2001; Martin, 2002; Martin, Huber Marshall, & Depry, 2001; Wandry & Repetto, 1993).

Change 2: Shift in Emphasis to Results

IDEA 2004 places greater emphasis on accountability of the educational system for improving transition outcomes for youths. IDEA 2004 modified the definition of transition from an "outcome-oriented process, which promotes movement from school to post-school activities" to a "results-oriented process, that is focused on improving the academic and functional achievement of the child to facilitate the child's movement from school to post-school activities . . ." (Sec. 614). IDEA 2004 requires that the student's IEP include ". . . appropriate measurable postsecondary goals based upon age appropriate transition assessments related to training, education, employment, and, where appropriate, independent living skills . . . and the transition services (including courses of study) needed to assist the child in reaching these goals" (IDEA 2004, Sec. 614). The challenge to implement appropriate transition services has become even more complex as general education reforms place increasing emphasis on academic performance for all students, including those with disabilities.

Change 3: An Exception to the Requirement to Evaluate the Student before a Change in Status

The 1997 law required a local educational agency to evaluate a student with a disability before there was a change in his or her eligibility status for special education (i.e., determined no longer to be a child with a disability). IDEA 2004 includes an exception to the 1997 requirement. For students who are (a) ending their eligibility due to graduation from secondary school with a regular diploma or (b) exceeding the age of eligibility for special education under state law, the school need not conduct such an evaluation. Instead, the LEA or district must provide the students with a "summary of academic achievement and functional performance, which shall include recommendations on how to assist the youth to meet their postsecondary goals" (Proposed Rules, Sec. 300.305(e)(3). The Summary of Performance (SOP) is discussed in detail in Chapter 11. A sample *SOP template* is provided in Appendix 3.

Change 4: Revision of "Statement of Interagency Responsibilities" in the IEP

The 1997 IDEA required that the IEP contain a "statement of needed transition services for the child, including, when appropriate, a statement of the interagency responsibilities or any needed linkages." The 2004 IDEA deletes this language in relation to transition services. However, the state preserves language under the definition of the IEP and its components requiring that the IEP include the

> . . . projected date for the beginning of services and modifications, the anticipated frequency, location and duration of those services [(D)(1)(A) (VII)]. . . . If a participating agency fails to provide the transition services described in the IEP, the local educational agency shall reconvene the IEP team to identify strategies to meet the transition objectives for the child set out in the IEP. [(D)(6)]

Interagency responsibility to provide needed services that support students' programs of study and postsecondary goals continues to be an expectation.

Change 5. Emphasis on Progress in the General Education Curriculum

The 2004 IDEA emphasizes the goal of enabling the student to access and make progress in the general education curriculum. In the development of the IEP, the IEP team is also required to consider special factors for children, including the following:

- *Behavior that impedes learning.* In the case of a child whose behavior interferes with his or her learning or that of others, consider appropriate strategies and supports, including positive behavioral interventions, to address that behavior.
- *Limited English proficiency.* In the case of a child with limited English proficiency, consider the language needs of the child as those needs relate to the child's IEP.
- *Braille needs.* In the case of a child who is blind or visually impaired, provide for instruction in Braille unless the IEP team determines that it is not appropriate for the child.
- *Communication needs.* Consider the communication needs of the child, and in the case of a child who is deaf or hard of hearing, consider the child's language and communication needs and opportunities for communication with others, along with the full range of needs.
- *Assistive technology.* Consider whether the child requires assistive technology services [Sec. 300.346(a)(2)].

Educators are asking how transition services "fit" within a standards-based educational system when the student is in the general education curriculum (see Chapter 10 discussion).

How Does NCLB Support Transition?

The No Child Left Behind Act of 2001 (NCLB, P.L. 107-110), first authorized as the Elementary and Secondary Education Act of 1965, also requires strategic cross-agency planning and collaboration to support students' transition from secondary education.

In 2002, the President's Commission on Excellence in Special Education (2002) issued a report with recommendations that dovetail with new requirements under NCLB that support collaboration and youth preparation for transition. Two of these recommendations in particular echo NCLB provisions that support youth transition.

1. *Mandate federal interagency collaboration to focus on transition services and to better coordinate services* to reach students with disabilities early. While funding for more focused transition services now exists, it is spread across multiple agencies, and the programs do not target transition services or foster coordination with other federal programs (p. 49). Second, increased federal enforcement of established interagency agreements is now required between state educational agencies (SEAs) and state vocational rehabilitation agencies (p. 49).

2. *Devote more attention to collaboration with families.* Families are the key to success for students with disabilities, and they need to be involved in all levels of decision making within schools (p. 38).

Several provisions in NCLB and the Rehabilitation Act mirror these recommendations and promote the transition of youths with disabilities and those at risk of school dropout. Appendix 2 presents the specific language of NCLB 2001 that supports transition for all youths.

NCLB Supports Transition for At-Risk Populations

At-risk youths are more likely than their peers to drop out of school, experience educational failure, or be involved in activities that are detrimental to their health and safety. Available research shows that children raised in economically disadvantaged families are at greater risk of low academic achievement, exhibit behavioral problems, have poor health, and have difficulties with adjustments to adulthood (Hale, 1998; Land & Legters, 2002). NCLB devotes Title I, Part D to prevention and intervention programs for children and youths who are neglected, delinquent, or at risk.

NCLB provides support for youths who are in transition out of institutions into home schools. Nearly one-third of the U.S. adult population does not advance beyond high school, and this proportion has remained relatively constant for nearly 30 years (Friedman, 2000). It is estimated that approximately one million youths per year leave school without completing their basic educational requirements (Barr & Parrett, 2001). Adolescents with emotional and behavioral disabilities (EBD) have only a 41.9 percent graduation rate and the highest dropout rate of any disability category (U.S. Department of Education, 2002).

Youths in Transition from Correctional Facilities

NCLB also strengthens transition services and supports for youths transferring into the community from correctional facilities such as adult jails, juvenile detention, less secure detention facilities, or protective shelters. The law strengthens the ability of youths exiting correctional facilities to enter postsecondary education or employment. Under NCLB, the school district is required to focus on the transition and academic needs of students returning from correctional facilities. Often there is a disconnect between the programs of local schools and correctional facilities, which results in low student achievement. As students transition from correctional facilities back to their local schools, follow-up services can ensure that their education continues and they can meet the same challenging state standards required of all students.

22

Youths with disabilities are substantially overrepresented in the juvenile justice system (Rutherford & Quinn, 1999). Youths with specific learning, emotional, or behavioral disabilities are more vulnerable to alternative placement outside their base school or in juvenile or adult corrections than youths not identified as disabled. Youths placed at risk for involvement in the juvenile justice system, including students with disabilities, must receive support and preventive services to minimize their vulnerability.

Women and Children in Poverty

Women and children account for more than three-quarters of households with incomes below the poverty level. Children from racial minority groups are much more likely to live in poverty than are white children. Unmarried teen mothers need access to day care, transportation, and other supports that will enable them to complete high school, enter employment, and pursue advanced education (National Council for Research on Women, 2001, 1998). NCLB focuses attention on the needs of women in poverty to assist them in completing high school and entering employment.

Transition Support for Native Americans

Native American students with disabilities face unique challenges to successful transition. Lack of familial support, chemical dependency, and lack of support networks for students with disabilities who enter higher education institutions all play a role in the high dropout rates and in the level of difficulty in making successful transitions into adulthood. Furthermore, other factors such as lack of employment opportunities, limited resources, and high poverty levels impede the ability of Native Americans to succeed in higher education and independent living. Unemployment rates run as high as 70 percent in some reservations, putting Native American youths, as a whole, at a heightened risk for failure to assume adult roles and responsibilities after leaving high school (Blasi, 2001; Leake, Kim-Rupnow, & Leung, 2003; Shafer & Rangasamy, 1995). NCLB devotes Title VII to Indian, Native Hawaiian, and Alaska Native education and support for career preparation and postsecondary education (Appendix 2).

How Does the Rehabilitation Act Support Transition?

Several provisions of the Rehabilitation Act address coordination with high schools to improve transition services for students who will be eligible for vocational rehabilitation (VR) services after leaving school.

The Rehabilitation Act Amendments of 1998 use essentially the same definition of transition services as that in IDEA.

The Rehabilitation Act requires cooperation with agencies responsible for transition of students from school to employment or postsecondary settings. This provision links the IEP and the Individual Written Rehabilitation Plan (IWRP) under the Rehabilitation Act to accomplish rehabilitation goals before high school graduation. The Rehabilitation Act also provides for ongoing support services that can include assessment of an employment situation at a worksite, skilled job trainers, job development and placement services, social skills training, or coordination of intensive services at the worksite or in the home that may be needed to maintain employment stability, independent living supports, and follow-up services.

Chapter 5

What Changes for Youths as They Move from Secondary to Postschool Environments?

Transition through high school to the postsecondary world is an exciting journey for the adolescent seeking to make new life choices. This passage can be a fragile one, however, for youths with disabilities who need additional support and preparation to make the journey. The completion of high school begins the passage into adult life, and there are several important changes that affect youths. The entitlement to special education services ends and young adults and their families are faced with a variety of choices about their future—employment, college, technical training, independent living, or military?

Post-High School Choices for Youths with Disabilities

The point of transition from high school to the postsecondary world is a challenging crossroad for all young people. They have to make choices about entering employment, whether they will apply to college, what they will study, where they will live, whether they will work while they study, and how they will pay for their living expenses. There are many postschool options for youths with disabilities in the United States.

- *Employment* in competitive work in a variety of skilled or semi-skilled occupations, or in supported work settings.
- *Career and technical colleges* offer a variety of options, including associate degrees, certificates, and work apprenticeships. Associate degree programs prepare students for technical occupations (e.g., accountant, dental hygienist, computer programmer). Technical diploma programs meet the needs of businesses and industry and provide employees with required certification for employment (e.g., automotive maintenance, accounting assistant, pharmacy technician). Apprenticeships are geared for individuals who are interested in working in industrial or service trades (e.g., carpentry, plumbing, machining).
- *Community colleges* are public, two-year colleges. They typically serve people in the surrounding communities and offer academic,

technical, and continuing education courses. The programs often lead to a license, a certificate, or an Associate of Arts or Science degree. Community colleges often operate under an *open admissions* policy, and admissions requirements may vary. Some community colleges offer programs for individuals with cognitive disabilities, autism, and other disabilities and are focused on developing functional and employment skills.

- *Four-year colleges and universities* offer a Bachelor of Arts or Bachelor of Science degree. Colleges and universities offer a wide variety of courses and resources from which to choose at undergraduate and graduate levels.
- *Military service* can also help young people achieve their career goals; however, the military branches are not required to accommodate individuals on the basis of disability (Brown, 2000; HEATH Resource Center, 2003).

For the youth planning to exit high school, what does he or she need to know about the differences between secondary and postsecondary settings? The inclusion of transition services in the student's IEP has contributed to improved planning for graduation and the world beyond high school. However, nationwide, recent research has pointed to the need to improve the quality of transition planning across the states to prepare students and families for the changes that occur once they leave secondary education (Storms, O'Leary, & Williams, 2000; Leake, 2003).

First, students with disabilities and their parents need to be better informed about the substantial differences in the rights and responsibilities of schools and students as they move from secondary school to the postsecondary world. The National Council on Disability noted

> . . . the lack of awareness among educators and parents regarding the policy contract between IDEA at the secondary level . . . and Section 504 at the post-secondary level. The result is that students are often harshly surprised rather than prepared for the disparity between the two levels of education . . . students themselves and parents are often "caught unaware" when the level of service provision drops off or is not automatically extended following high school. (2003, p. 8)

In elementary and secondary school, the teachers and other school professionals share the responsibility for the educational success with the student, but *in higher education it is up to the individual.* Students must possess the skills to advocate for their needs in college or on the job, skills they may not have learned in high school. Table 5.1 summarizes the changes students can expect as they navigate the transition from secondary to postsecondary environments.

TABLE 5.1 *Summary of Changes from Secondary to Postsecondary Environments*

Secondary Setting	Postsecondary Setting
• Entitled to accommodations	• No entitled services
• Entitled to IEP and specialized services	• Student must self-disclose disability
• IEP team shapes the student's program	• Student must self-advocate for services
• Families shape the decisions about courses of study and services	• Student must prove disability
• Evaluations are provided	• Student must know own strengths and limitations

Self-Advocacy Skills Needed for Postsecondary Participation: It's Up to the Student

Only one-half of secondary schools have specific curriculum to teach secondary students *self-advocacy and self-determination skills* (GAO, 2003; U.S. Department of Education, 2004b). However, most states are now emphasizing transition services in their statewide improvement plans and are working toward ensuring that all students with disabilities who need such services are provided with adequate planning and support. Postsecondary education is different from secondary school in many ways. Class schedules are more flexible, class offerings are more varied, and class periods are shorter. Students are expected to take full responsibility for their progress and to spend much more time and effort on independent study. For students living on campus, there is a variety of social opportunities and a sense of freedom from parental supervision. Postsecondary school is not free—as is public secondary school—and books can be very costly. Students must be prepared for the changes associated with the legal status of being an adult.

Age of Majority: Transfer of Rights to the Student

Age of majority refers to the age at which a young person acquires all the rights and responsibilities of being an adult. In most states the age is 18. IDEA 1997 and 2004 outlined a procedure for the transfer of parental rights to the student when he or she reaches the age of majority. Collaboration and communication between school professionals and parents is essential. Schools must now notify the student and both parents about the student's rights when he or she reaches the age of majority. One year before the student reaches the age of majority under state law, the IEP must include a statement that he or she has been *informed of the rights that transfer* to the student once he or she reaches the age of majority. This transfer of rights is an enormous step toward the student's independence and participation in the decision making for further education and future planning (Bremer, Kachgal, & Schoeller, 2003; Eisenman & Chamberlin, 2001). It is important that students and parents have opportunities to understand the impact of this responsibility.

> The change in the role of families is dramatic as a student graduates high school and leaves the coverage of IDEA—the student's family is no longer legally responsible for the student, but they switch from being a legal advocate to being an "encourager" or coach of a student. Family involvement is essential for students advancing to postsecondary education. During college, we need encouragers. One of the disabilities support providers put it this way: "Families need to be the rah-rah section." And then as people move through to employment, families still need to be supporters. The role changes as those environments change, but is still critical. (Stodden & Welley, 2002)

Family collaboration must be a centerpiece in transition preparation activities for students with special needs.

Laws Governing Secondary and Postsecondary College Settings Are Different: Section 504

For students with disabilities, the laws governing special services and support in the postsecondary setting are different and affect students' experiences in many ways. Examples of these changes include the following:

1. While high school decision making is parent-driven, students in the postsecondary setting are responsible for identifying their disability, providing documentation, and requesting assistance (student-driven).
2. Disability services personnel make decisions about services based on the "reasonable accommodations" requirements of the Americans with Disabilities act (ADA) and Section 504 of the Rehabilitation Act, and not on services prescribed by the Individuals with Disabilities Education Act (IDEA).
3. Students are offered a menu of service choices but there is no team of people who meet and decide for them (though there are counselors to provide guidance and information).
4. Students with disabilities often have to repeat the process of requesting accommodations each new semester from the disability support services office.
5. Students may have to renegotiate accommodations each new semester with new professors or instructors (NCSET, 2004).

In the postsecondary setting, supports and accommodations are based on what is "reasonable" to help the student access the content and reduce barriers to learning. Unlike supportive services under IDEA, they are not designed specifically to promote student achievement. For example, a college is more likely to provide a note-taker for the student than a tutor.

Postsecondary services under Section 504 of the Rehabilitation Act of 1973 are not mandated by law as an entitlement for all students as are services in high school, but rather are based on whether (1) the individual is determined to be eligible for the services, and (2) whether the accommodation does not result in a change in content or standards expected for all students. An *accommodation* is defined as a support or service that is provided to help a student fully access the college curriculum, course, or classroom. Students with impaired spelling or handwriting skills, for example, may be accommodated by a note-taker or permission to take class notes on a laptop computer. An accommodation does not change the content of what is being taught or the expectation that the student meet a performance standard applied for all students. A *modification* is defined as a change to the curriculum or other material being taught, which alters the standards or expectations for students with disabilities. Instruction can be modified so that the material is presented differently and the expectations of what the student will master are changed. Modifications are not allowed in most postsecondary education environments (Scott, Shaw, & McGuire, 2006). *Assistive technology* is defined as any device that helps a student function in a given environment, but does not limit the device to expensive or "high-tech" options (Center for Applied Special Technology, 2004).

"Proving" the Presence of a Disability

At the postsecondary level, students also may have to prove their disability in order to qualify for services (Gaylord, Johnson, Lehr, Bremer, & Hasazi, 2004). Postsecondary educational institutions do not typically accept an Individualized Education Program (IEP) from a high school as documentation of a disability or need for an academic accommodation (for an excellent discussion of documentation of disability see HEATH Resource Center's Counselor Toolkit, 2006). According to the Office of Civil Rights, U.S. Department of Justice (2002):

> You must inform the college that you have a disability, and need an academic adjustment. Unlike your school district (in secondary school), your post-secondary school is not required to identify you as having a disability or assess your needs.

Colleges, however, may be able to use high school testing results, if the information is current and disability-specific. For example, after consultation with the college, a student with a learning disability might submit the psychoeducational evaluation from eleventh grade as *documentation of the learning disability*. If a student needs additional documentation, it is the student's responsibility to obtain it. It is very important that students collect and maintain their high school records for the purposes of disability documentation (Hart, Zafft, & Zimbrich, 2001; Shaw & Dukes, 2001). A discussion of new high school documentation requirements under IDEA can be found in Chapter 11.

Despite the challenges of entering the "different world" of postsecondary education, recent laws have greatly improved access and support of youths with disabilities. Most postsecondary institutions are responding to new legal mandates and developing greater capacity to recruit and to include students with a full range of disabilities. Collaboration among special and general educators, related services professionals, school psychologists and counselors is essential in providing adequate documentation of disability and preparation for transition to help graduates access postsecondary education and employment.

Chapter 6

What Is Transition under IDEA?
A Comprehensive Planning Process

What Does IDEA 2004 Require?

Chapter 4 summarized the changes in IDEA 1997 and 2004 that have affected transition services. This chapter will examine transition definitions and requirements under IDEA 2004. The term "transition services" under IDEA 2004 means a "coordinated set of activities" for students that:

1. Is designed within a results-oriented process, which promotes movement from school to post-school activities, including post-secondary education, vocational training, integrated employment (including supported employment), continuing and adult education, adult services, independent living, or community participation;
2. Is based upon the individual student's strengths, taking into account the student's preferences and interests; and
3. Includes instruction, related services, community experiences, the development of employment and other post-school adult living objectives, and, when appropriate, acquisition of daily living skills and functional vocational evaluation. (IDEA 2004, Sec. 602)

The IEP, beginning no later than the first IEP in effect when the student is 16 and updated annually, must include a statement of "appropriate measurable postsecondary goals based on age appropriate transition assessments related to training, education, employment and independent living skills" (IDEA 2004, Sec. 614). Students' success will depend on their active participation in setting postsecondary goals and planning a coordinated set of services to achieve those goals.

IDEA 2004 Paradox:
Backward Planning for Transition

Implementing effective transition at age 16 (or earlier) involves processes far more complex than those defined in the law. Several facilitative implementation processes are key to achieving effective transition and ensuring adequate planning for students to get them ready for the final stage of transition—the exit from high school. Facilitative

31

processes mean practices that state and local educational agencies have
developed over the years as a result of their students' experiences with
transition under IDEA and their own evaluation of services (Repetto,
2006). These practices are longer-term, comprehensive processes of
decision making that:

1. Begin as the student prepares to exit middle school and make
   decisions and choices about the high school course of study;
2. Involve assistance with the adjustment to high school;
3. Involve IEP planning that defines a postsecondary goal and designs
   a course of study, supportive and supplemental services, and a
   variety of transition-related activities that support the postsecondary
   goal (Sec. 614). It is the "course of study" requirement in IDEA that
   connects transition with curriculum standards and assessment for all
   students.
4. Prepare the student and family to take an active role in planning
   during high school and the student to take responsibility for his or
   her own future upon exit from high school (self-determination and
   self-advocacy).

As Steven Covey (2004) advised, "begin with the end in mind."
Applying this idea for transition, the student and the IEP team conducts a
careful backward planning process with a clear eye to the final outcome—the postsecondary goal. Figure 6.1 depicts the long-range
transition planning process that many local districts are developing.

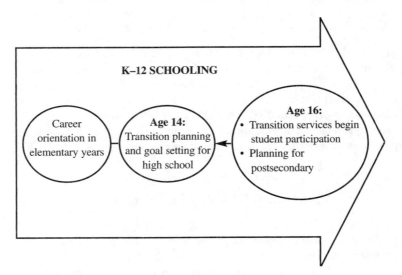

FIGURE 6.1 *Backward Planning for Transition*

32

In the words of one high school student:

> I was asked to lead my own IEP meeting where we talked about "transition" and my plans for graduation. My teacher helped me plan for it and what to expect. I felt like I was in charge of my own future and everyone was listening to what I was interested in. Now I was leading something important. And that's the way it should be.

Transition Is a Comprehensive and Individualized Planning Process: Applying Universal Design

Universal design for learning (UDL), a concept that emerged from the field of architecture, is an approach to designing products and environments for maximum usability by a diverse population. Ramped entrances and automatic doors are architectural examples of Universal Design (Center for Applied Special Technology, 2004; Smith & Leconte, 2004). In educational settings, *universal design* means that environments and curricula are designed to be flexible and usable by students of widely varying abilities. Universal design provides a way to offer flexible curriculum and learning environments so that students with widely varying abilities all have the opportunity to access the general curriculum (and assessments) and achieve the academic content standards that have been established for all students in the school (Caspar & Leuchovius, 2005).

In the past, providing "access" to general education has meant *enabling physical access* to the classroom and, for some students, the provision of adaptive equipment to facilitate sensory and motor access to the curriculum. More recently, however, there has been a growing interest in *designing curriculum, instruction, and assessment* so as to increase access and reduce the need for individualized adaptation and accommodation (Casper & Leuchovius, 2005). In secondary education, in order for students with disabilities to have meaningful access to and make progress in the general curriculum, transition planning and services must be integrated. To meet the criteria of *flexible and widely usable curricula and environments,* the UDL framework, applied to transition, must:

- Recognize different pathways to graduation for students requiring flexible planning timetables;
- Incorporate the concept of integrated transition planning and participation in a general education course of study;
- Recognize the need for flexible combinations of academic, career-vocational classes, and community-based work experiences to achieve different pathways to graduation.

For some students with disabilities, the typical planning process for application for work or to a two- or four-year college proceeds much the same way as it does for students without disabilities. However, for many students with disabilities, decisions about postsecondary choices are often complex and require long-term advanced planning. Approaches to transition planning and service delivery will, of course, vary for students with different disabilities. Transition services, therefore, are *tailored to the individual needs of the student and their postsecondary goals.* Transition services can be clustered into pathways or service patterns that are arranged to meet the needs of students with different long-term goals. These pathways vary by level of support, type and emphasis of curriculum, type of assessments, and expected postschool placement and service needs. A pathways approach also provides a framework for examining student needs and goals early in their educational program, long before graduation is upon them, and developing a course of preparation to achieve those goals. While some students may need time-limited transition supports and some may need ongoing services, the transition planning process for students with disabilities should begin early, as they enter secondary education. For students without disabilities, such long-range vision and secondary planning to achieve postsecondary goals is the *typical model* that begins as the student exits from middle school and makes choices for a high school course of study. Table 6.1 presents an example of pathways and levels of support for students with different postsecondary goals.

TABLE 6.1   *Pathways and Levels of Support in Transition*

Path/Level	Domains Emphasized	Assessments Used	Degree of Self-Determination	Expected Outcome or Exit Goal
1 Academic	Academic	Academic/ standardized	High	College enrollment
2 Career-Technical Training	Vocational & Social	Vocational & community-based "authentic" assessments	High	Vocational-technical school or apprenticeship
3 Employment	Social & Independent Living	Vocational assessments in authentic or simulated settings	High to moderate	Employment
4 Supported Setting	Social & Independent Living	Social, adaptive behavior, and independent living skills assessments	Moderate and assisted	Supported employment and supervised living

Source: Greene, G., & Kochhar-Bryant, C. (2003). *Pathways to successful transition for youth with disabilities* (pp. 199–229). Columbus, OH: Merrill Prentice-Hall.

Transition, as required by IDEA 2004, represents an individualized flexible planning process, offering a spectrum of services and choices for youths who have separate and individual needs. Transition is fully consistent with the concept of *universal design* for learning environments.

Understanding a "Coordinated Set of Activities" under IDEA

The systematic, cumulative, and long-range nature of transition planning and the decision-making process is implied but not made explicit in IDEA statutory language, and is not well implemented in the states. IDEA 1997 amendments redefined transition services as a "coordinated set of activities aimed at a specific student outcome (e.g., employment, referral to rehabilitation services, enrollment in college); activities which promote the movement of a student from school to post-school activities which may include post-secondary education, vocational training, integrated employment (including supported employment), continuing and adult education, adult services, independent living, or community participation" (Sec. 602(34)(A)). The coordinated set of activities (above) must be (a) based on the individual student's strengths, preferences, and interests, and (b) include needed activities in the areas of instruction, community experiences, the development of employment and other postschool adult living objectives, and, if appropriate, daily living skills and functional vocational evaluation.

The word "coordinated" is the only reference—and an oblique one—to a *systematic approach* to transition. The term was first defined in the regulations for the 1990 IDEA (P.L. 101-476) to mean both "(1) the linkage between each of the component activities that comprise transition services, and (2) the interrelationship between the various agencies that are involved in the provision of transition services to a student" (U.S. Department of Education, 1992, p. 48644). Thus, the various transition activities must complement and be coordinated with each other, and the different agencies responsible for providing the services must do the same, making sure that the services they provide to the student meet, in a coordinated, nonduplicating fashion, his or her transition needs. Because the transition process relies on the involvement of many individuals and many service providers, this coordination of effort is essential. Transition, viewed as a systematic, individualized process that incorporates a "coordinated set of activities":

1. Is a continuous process through transition from middle school and through high school;

2. Incorporates a coordination strategy that provides continuity of planning and links each student with a transition coordinator, counselor, or ombudsman;
3. Considers students' anticipated postsecondary goals;
4. Is a long-range planning and decision-making framework for students and families that addresses a variety of domains of education and life preparation;
5. Addresses curriculum options, including participation in the general education curriculum, career-technical, community-based learning, nonacademic learning activities, and standardized assessments;
6. Incorporates related and supportive services (opportunities) identified by students, parents, and professionals;
7. Incorporates the coordination of appropriate community-based and adult service agencies, vocational rehabilitation, health and mental health agencies, postsecondary institutions, and employment development services.

Transition planning is foundational for the IEP planning process. Long-term transition planning provides an overarching framework that guides the development of the IEP and provides continuity in the process about the immediate and long-term future of the student (Kochhar-Bryant & Bassett, 2003). It is a blueprint for direction setting and for constructing a plan that is aimed at high school exit goals most appropriate for the individual. The transition plan is vital to accessing and progressing in the secondary education curriculum because it defines specific needs and services in regard to the secondary curriculum and associated assessments, related services, and supports. While IDEA 2004 moves the starting point for transition services once again to age 16, many states are choosing to continue their practices of early planning (begun under IDEA 1997) to initiate planning when the student turns 14.

Determining Needed Transition Services: Use of Assessment in Transition

IDEA does not prescribe how the IEP team should determine the kinds of transition services a student needs. However, the law requires that transition services be included as a component of the IEP using the same process that is used to identify other needed educational or related services. According to IDEA 2004, decisions about transition services must be based on students' strengths, preferences, and interests. It is, therefore, implied in IDEA that there will be a process in place to assess these *strengths, preferences, and interests.* Transition assessments were defined by Clark (1998) as "the appropriate multiple assessments for particular transitions throughout life" (p. 1). Transition assessment in special education is person-centered and emphasizes *individual capabilities* rather than disabilities. Traditional assessment in special education has been criticized for focusing too heavily upon student weaknesses rather than strengths (Greene & Kochhar-Bryant, 2003, pp. 232–233). An effective assessment process for secondary youths addresses transition issues in several life domains, asking questions such as the following:

- What knowledge and skills does the student need to successfully enter employment, postsecondary education, adult services, independent living, or community participation?
- What knowledge and skills does the student currently demonstrate in each of these areas?
- What knowledge and skills does the student still need to acquire over the next few years?

This information will be crucial for identifying the appropriate transition services that match the student's long-range postsecondary goal. The transition plan should be aimed at the knowledge and skill areas that the student most needs to strengthen in order to prepare for transition (Flexer, Simmons, Luft, & Baer, 2001; Smith & Leconte, 2004). The transition plan should also address skills in the range of life domains that are relevant to the student's postsecondary goals.

Transition assessments can help students understand their interests and preferences in relation to their academic education, career-vocational, and postsecondary environments (Flexer, Simmons, Luft, & Baer, 2001). To obtain the broadest picture of students' strengths, interests, and preferences, a variety of tests or measures must be used. Such information about the student can be obtained through observations of the student; anecdotal information from teachers, parents, students, standardized tests, and other informal assessments (Neubert, 2003).

For example, achievement tests used in the classroom can contribute information about the student's skills in reading, math, or other subject areas. Psychometric tests can be used to measure the attributes of the individual such as his or her interests, personality, or aptitudes. Observations of the student also contribute valuable information about the student, such as attentiveness, dexterity, attitude, and skill levels on particular tasks. Particularly useful observational and anecdotal information about the student comes from students and parents, because they are closest to the student and most familiar with their skills in a variety of settings.

While achievement and psychometric testing and observations provide useful information, they may not provide sufficient information for planning nonacademic goals. Systematic vocational assessment of students is, therefore, strongly recommended (Leconte & Neubert, 1997; Neubert, 2003; Sitlington & Neubert, 1998; Smith & Leconte, 2004). Through the assessment process, students and families learn about a variety of careers, as well as the student's personal and vocational strengths and needs. Vocational assessment should also gather information that is not available through academic testing—specifically the essential characteristics of the individual that make up his or her vocational profile, including the student's:

- Occupational or vocational interests and preferences;
- Aptitudes in skills such as mechanical, spatial, numerical, and clerical;
- Worker style preferences, such as the desire to work with people or things;
- Learning preferences and styles, such as auditory, visual, or hands-on exposure;
- Worker characteristics, including student traits, values, employability skills, and other work-related behaviors;
- Abilities in specific technical, industrial, or other skills required in actual jobs; and
- Functional or life skills, needed to address personal and independent living problems such as transportation, financial and housing management, and social skills (Leconte & Neubert, 1997; Neubert, 2003; Rothenbacher & Leconte, 1990).

This kind of information can be gathered through informal means such as inventories that measure interests, learning styles, and worker characteristics. Additional assessment approaches involve having students perform tasks that simulate the actual skills needed in a particular job, or perform tasks in actual workplace settings. The process of collecting information about the student in a variety of transition domains is known as ecological assessment (Bulgren & Knackendoffel, 1986).

This method involves looking closely at the environment where an activity normally takes place and determining through observation the actual steps involved in performing the activity (e.g., at a worksite or on a bus). Whatever the methods used in assessment, the end result should be a deeper and more comprehensive understanding of the student's skills and readiness for the postschool environment. Such understanding should lead to more appropriate decisions about transition goals and services that are sensitive to the student's interests, preferences, and aptitudes (Greene, 2003; Neubert, 2003).

Chapter 7

How Does the IEP Team Help the Student Prepare for Transition?

The IEP Team

Each public school child who receives special education and related services must have an Individualized Education Program (IEP). IEP planning is designed to be a coordinated process among professionals and programs within the school, and often between schools and community service agencies, as students progress through the secondary years and prepare for transition to postsecondary settings. The IEP team includes the following participants: (1) the student and his or her parents; (2) at least one regular education teacher of such child (if the child is, or may be, participating in the general education classroom); (3) at least one special education teacher; (4) a representative of the local educational agency that is providing services to the child; (5) an individual who can interpret the instructional implications of evaluation results; and (6) individuals invited by the parents who have knowledge or special expertise regarding the child, including related services personnel (IDEA, 2004).

The child's regular education teacher is also a member of the IEP team and should participate in the development of the IEP. His or her participation may include determining the need for appropriate positive behavioral interventions and strategies; determining supplementary aids, services, and program modifications; and support for school personnel.

For students who have two- or four-year colleges as their postsecondary goal, the courses that they take in their final years should not only meet requirements for graduating from secondary school, but also for entering postsecondary education. The team identifies and explores the academic or career-technical-academic program and types of supports and accommodations that the student will need in postsecondary environments and plans for ways to prepare the student to transition to these supports (NCSET, 2004). For students with a postsecondary goal of employment, the team identifies academic, career-focused courses and community-based work experiences needed to qualify for employment in the chosen career area.

Role of the Student

The student should be integral to the process of developing his or her IEP/transition plan and should be prepared to participate in meetings to the extent possible. The student is the focal point of transition planning. To the extent of the student's abilities, he or she should be prepared for and assisted in leading the meeting. These experiences help the youth develop *self-determination skills* and accept greater responsibility for planning for the future. The role of the student on the IEP team is to:

- Prepare for the IEP team meetings and identify individuals who would like to participate in the team meeting.
- With support and preparation, take a leadership and decision-making role in team discussions, and with practice and support, learn to lead their own IEP meetings.
- Identify personal strengths, preferences, interests, and needs. The student may discuss these or may demonstrate them through a portfolio, written resume, video resume, or with pictures or other visuals.
- Identify and discuss preferences for supportive services, accommodations, and modifications needed to progress academically, vocationally, and in the community.
- Assume the age of majority rights at 18 (unless the state has set a different age), or unless exempted from assuming age of majority rights by a court-appointed guardian.

Role of the Parents and Family Members

Parents and family members keep the IEP team grounded and focused on the student's needs and goals. They actively participate in finding essential support services and in developing the transition component of the Individualized Education Program. The parents' and family members' role in the partnership is to:

- Prepare the student for meaningful participation in the IEP process.
- Provide information about the student's postsecondary and career interests, strengths, support needs, and independent living skills.
- Engage in all aspects of the IEP planning, discussion, and decision making.
- Identify friends, family, and members of community support services who should participate in the IEP team meetings.
- Participate in referrals to transition programs and adult services (e.g., vocational rehabilitation services, developmental disabilities services, community mental health services).
- Along with the student, follow up on services that are provided by community-based agencies.
- Locate information on local and state disability support resources such as those under the Social Security Administration (Supplemental Security Income), Medicaid, transportation resources, and trust funds for long-term in-home or community residential supports.

Role of the Local Educational Agency (LEA)

The school district is the primary coordinator and provider of transition services for students with disabilities receiving special education. The LEA's role in the transition system is to:

- Prepare students and parents/families for leadership roles in the Individualized Education Program process.
- Prepare all students for successful transition to responsible and productive adult lives in the community.
- Assist students to determine their preferences, strengths, and needs related to postsecondary goals.
- Provide information to families and students on students' progress in achieving their current IEP goals.
- Provide teachers with training, resources, and collaboration time to design instruction, accommodations, and modifications for students with disabilities in special and general education.
- Suggest courses of study and work experiences related to the students' interests and postsecondary goals.
- Assist students, parents/families, and IEP teams to write statements of needed transition services in the IEP that are appropriate for the student's postsecondary goal.
- Assist students and parents/families to identify and link with related and community-based services to facilitate the movement from school to postsecondary settings and the adult service system.
- Coordinate professionals, agencies, services, or programs for students during the transition process.
- Advocate for transition services at the individual student and system levels (adapted from Grossi, Schaaf, Steigerwald, & Thomas, 2000).

What Professionals Collaborate in Transition Planning?

Constructive communication and collaboration among professionals and families are essential as the student prepares to transition from secondary to postsecondary settings, work, and adult life. A variety of school personnel participate in the planning and delivery of transition services. School personnel include the following:

Principal/Administrator

The principal provides leadership and guidance in developing transition services and support to teachers, students, and parents. Principals can affect the quality of all aspects of transition services, including staff preparation for transition coordination, interagency collaboration, student and family participation, and data collection on transition outcomes. Such leadership can make the difference between minimal transition services and an effective collaborative "system."

General Education Teacher, Career Vocational Teacher, Special Education Teacher

The teacher's role and responsibility is to provide academic and social skills instruction in the secondary setting and to build students' connections through community-based experiences. Such instruction also includes self-determination and self-advocacy skills to help students understand and be able to (a) discuss their abilities and disabilities; and (b) advocate for needed accommodations or modifications in the postsecondary environment.

The Transition Coordinator or Service Coordinator

The transition coordinator's role is to assist students with postsecondary planning and to link students and families to school and community resources. Each school system may define the role of the transition coordinator differently. Secondary transition coordinators or service coordinators typically begin work with students when they reach the age at which they are eligible for services and planning (16 under IDEA 2004, and 14–15 in many local education agencies). Recent research on the role of transition coordinators shows that 94 percent of states also employ one or more at the state level (Jackson, 2003; Schiller et al., 2003; U.S. Department of Education, 2003).

The coordinator works with the student to identify preferences and short- and long-range goals. He or she collaborates with general educators to recommend a course of study through high school to prepare for careers and independent living in either college or employment settings. The coordinator arranges opportunities for the student (or a group of students) to learn about different careers through videos, job shadowing, visits to work environments, and hands-on work activities that allow the student(s) to try out a job. Finally the coordinator makes connections with the adult service system, identifies the support services or accommodations the student may need in the postsecondary setting, assists students to assemble portfolios of academic records, job experiences, resumes, and postsecondary recommendations. Transition coordinators may follow up with the student and continue their support services for a period of time after the student has graduated.

In many local communities there is a cadre of coordinators who function at individual and interagency levels. They perform activities that impact students and the service system as a whole in broad ways, including:

- *Increasing transition service access to target groups:* Improving transition services for students who could not participate without special accommodations and support.
- *Affecting service priorities and service distribution:* Providing assessment and referral of students to ensure that they are given priority, acting as gatekeepers for access to services and as the "eyes and ears" of the system to communicate student needs to decision makers.
- *Enhancing communication across agencies and disciplines:* Using a common language for sharing information about individuals in the service system, they assess transition service needs at the inter-agency level and assist with communication among service agencies.
- *Providing quality assurance and monitoring:* Integrating local, state, and federal transition laws and guidelines and helping agencies adhere to guidelines related to service quality; monitoring the delivery of interagency transition services.
- *Conducting interagency problem solving:* Intervening in interagency conflicts; seeking alternative services as needed, intervening in human rights issues, trouble-shooting interagency conflicts and procedural barriers.
- *Monitoring service costs:* Procuring transition-related services for individual students and, in some systems, controlling a support budget for allocation to individuals (Kochhar-Bryant, 2003; Kochhar, West, & Taymans, 2000).

School Counselor and Guidance Counselor

High school counselors implement counseling programs and provide a variety of supports. *Classroom guidance* involves helping students develop academic skills, including organizational, study, and test-taking skills. They assist with postsecondary planning and college application process. Counselors help students understand themselves and others, develop peer relationships and effective social skills, communication skills, and coping strategies. They help students with *individual planning* by guiding them to develop academic plans, career plans, and transition plans. They assist students in scheduling classes to meet academic requirements that are consistent with their career goals. High school counselors are professional educators with a mental health perspective who are integral to the total educational program for youths in high school.

School Psychologist

The psychologist conducts psychoeducational testing for students suspected of having educational disabilities and evaluation, including individualized intelligence testing, achievement testing, and assessments of visual perception and motor and social/ emotional disabilities. School psychologists also provide consultation in educational planning, make instructional recommendations, and make recommendations to teachers and parents for restructuring students' schedules within the school.

Occupational Therapist, Physical Therapist, Speech Therapist and Nurse

These related services professionals assist students with physical and special health care needs during the transition process. They provide consultation to the teachers, transition coordinators, employment specialists, and employers on work-related tasks and skill performance that may be affected by the student's physical disability, health care needs, or communication skills. School nurses communicate health needs to other school personnel and explain the implications of medical conditions for students' participation in school activities.

School Assistance Counselors and Resource Officers

Some secondary schools employ school student assistance counselors who provide prevention/intervention services for students who may be at risk for substance abuse or behavioral problems. The student assistance counselor serves as a member of the overall student personnel team and assists in the identification of at-risk students. Student assistance counselors provide individual and group counseling in school, as well as follow-up communication with families. They serve as a resource for identifying outpatient and hospital facilities to assist children and families in securing appropriate community-based assistance. The School Resource Officer (SRO) provides a police presence at the school and assists in ensuring a safe school environment. The purpose of having the presence of an SRO in the secondary school is to proactively identify and address potentially unsafe situations.

Vocational Rehabilitation Counselor

Vocational Rehabilitation (VR) is a federally funded program designed to assist individuals with disabilities to prepare for, secure, or maintain employment. The vocational rehabilitation counselor provides information to members of the IEP team about VR services and student eligibility upon exiting high school, writes an *Individual Plan for Employment* (IPE) for eligible students, provides support during initial employment, and coordinates individualized employment services as needed to maintain the job.

Chapter 8

How Is the Transition Plan Developed?

While IDEA 2004 no longer requires it, the law allows state and local educational agencies to continue to provide early transition planning for students who need it. Many states, such as New York and Massachusetts, already have structures in place for early transition planning and are choosing to continue to begin the process for many students at age 14 or 15. Most states also recognize different pathways to graduation for students, which *necessitate individualized planning processes and timetables* for students who may need more services and supports. The following sections describe transition planning in two stages, at ages 14–15 and age 16.

Writing the Transition Component in the IEP: Phase 1, Ages 14–15

At age 14 the student's postsecondary goals should be developed and transition service needs identified. The needs will include a course of study and a year-by-year plan to achieve transition goals. The IEP team must determine what instruction and educational experiences will help the student prepare for transition from high school to postsecondary life. When the student turns 14, the IEP includes transition-related content in the following areas:

- *Postschool goal statements:* Address desired postschool employment, two- or four-year college or technical training, and aspirations for independent living and community participation.

- *Present levels of performance:* Include a summary assessment of the student's long-range transition service needs, identifying the skills necessary to succeed in the secondary environment and to prepare for transition to postsecondary and community living.

- *Goals and objectives:* Include specific instructional services related to developing transition skills and self-determination skills to understand one's abilities and participate in the IEP planning process.

- *Related services:* Include supportive services needed to develop transition skills, knowledge, and abilities.

- *Coordinated set of activities:* Addresses educational programming that matches the student's transition goals and objectives with the course of study and class schedule. The coordinated set of activities:

  a. Summarizes what the school will do during this annual IEP period to help the student achieve the stated outcomes.

  b. Indicates skills and experiences, not elsewhere included in the IEP, that the school will provide to prepare the student for adult life.

  c. Indicates who will provide coordination and follow-along to ensure the student is receiving the services or supports stated in his or her IEP.

O'Leary and Collision (2002) defined at least six potential areas in the coordinated set of activities (although others can be identified, if needed, for the student):

- Academic and career-vocational instruction
- Related services and supports
- Community work or service experiences
- Employment and postsecondary activities
- Functional or daily living and social skills
- Transition assessments or functional vocational evaluation

The statement of coordinated set of activities should clearly identify what the school will do in concrete and realistic terms. For example, "the IEP coordinator will assist Shawn to explore career opportunities in the music recording and production industry." These statements focus the activities of the school-based team (teacher, guidance counselor, psychologist, transition coordinator, mental health counselor, and others relevant professionals) for each student. The activities of each team member should contribute to helping the student achieve the goals and objectives identified in the IEP. These activities should be stated in terms that are measurable and concrete so that it is easy to determine whether they have been performed. The coordinated set of activities refers to what the school (and relevant professionals) will do to assist the student; they are *different from the short-term objectives for what the* student *will accomplish.* Such a short-term objective for Shawn might be stated as follows: "Shawn will work with the guidance counselor in the first quarter to identify at least three community colleges in the region that have music recording programs."

Writing the Transition Component in the IEP: Phase 2, Age 16 and Beyond

According to IDEA 2004, needed transition services must be included in the first IEP that is in effect once the student reaches age 16. Transition services could include instruction and related services, community experiences, vocational evaluation, employment, and other activities involved in adult living. A statement of interagency responsibilities should also be included as well as needed links to other agency services. The IEP team should also monitor the student's high school program to be sure the student completes all graduation requirements that are identified as appropriate to the student's postsecondary goal. Transition related content in the IEP includes the following:

- *Postsecondary goal statements:* Address desired postsecondary employment, two- or four-year college or technical training, community living aspirations.
- *Present levels of performance:* Identify the skills necessary for educational success in the secondary environment, as well as in the workplace, community participation, and independent living.
- *Goals and objectives:* Include specific instructional services related to development of transition skills and development of self-determination skills to actively participate in the IEP planning process (and lead meetings, if possible).
- *Related and community-based services:* Including school-based and community services necessary to participate in secondary and transition curriculum. Participating agencies are those that will collaborate with the school to jointly develop a transition service plan and provide transition services for the student. For example, for some students the school develops the IEP/transition component and the vocational rehabilitation agency develops an Individualized Plan for Employment (IPE). An agency should be included in the IEP only if it has agreed to perform a specific transition activity or service for the student. At a minimum, the information on the participating agency that should be included in the IEP is agency name, contact person, telephone (e-mail, also), service being delivered, and implementation date of services.
- *Coordinated set of activities:* Aligns the course of study and course schedule with needed transition services, addressing instruction, community-based learning experiences, employment, related and community services, activities of daily living, and functional vocational evaluation (when appropriate).

47

Writing Postsecondary Goal Statements

Postsecondary goal statements are statements of "measurable postsecondary goals based on transition assessments" (IDEA, 2004, Sec. 614). They may also be looked at as destination, or "future" statements, based upon the student's vision and hopes for the future. Although the word "measurable" is included in the IDEA language, these statements are *not* the same as behavioral objectives or contractual guarantees. While the wording for such broad goal statements may be "soft" (e.g., the student is "working toward," "hopes to," "desires to prepare for"), the transition goals and objectives (what the school or cooperating agencies will specifically do) designed to prepare him or her for the goal should be very specific. Postsecondary goal statements should:

1. Identify what the student's goals and dreams are in the areas of employment, continuing education, and community living.
2. Identify why the particular postsecondary goal makes sense for this student.
3. Identify the path (set of coordinated transition activities) required to achieve the postsecondary goal.

There should be *at least* one outcome statement in each of the areas that is developed in collaboration with the student and family. Postsecondary goal statements written in the three areas should address the following questions:

- *Employment:* Will the student become part of the workforce?
- *Postsecondary education:* Will the student go on for further education, such as a two- or four-year college, career-technical school, adult education, skill improvement workshops, armed forces, or formal apprenticeship?
- *Community living:* How will the student participate in the community (e.g., independent living, transportation, recreation, civic activities, relationships, etc.)? (Adapted from New York State Department of Education, 2005; O'Leary & Collision, 2002).

Linking the Transition Goals and Objectives to the Educational Program (Course of Study)

Once transition goals and objectives have been developed for a student, transition activities and the course of study are then designed to help the student achieve those goals. Courses should relate directly to the student's postsecondary goals, increasing the chances the student will be invested in his or her program of study. Courses of study for many students with disabilities match those of the general population.

For students with moderate or severe disabilities, courses of study are likely to be different. Instead of listing specific course titles, for students with moderate to severe disabilities one should list general content areas (e.g., mobility, self-determination, independent living, money management, personal relationships) (O'Leary & Collision, 2002). For example, the student may need to strengthen basic math skills and learn to apply them in a work setting. This can be accomplished by blending academic course work with vocational education. Investigating supervised community living opportunities to address the student's independent living domain, however, is an activity that falls outside the typical curriculum. The community is necessarily the site of many transition activities.

For a student with a mild disability, an example of the desired postschool outcomes and the resulting course of study might look like this:

Postschool Outcome/Vision

Employment:	I would like to become a social worker, like the kind who helps kids who have been abused or neglected.
Community Participation:	I enjoy cooking for my parents and would like to volunteer making food baskets and serving meals to the homeless.
Recreation & Leisure:	I want to learn more about yoga and Tai Chi. I enjoy spending time outdoors with my friends playing Frisbee and soccer.
Postsecondary Training & Learning Opportunities:	I want to start out at a community college taking classes that will prepare me for a four-year university and then apply to a four-year college to get a degree in social work.
Independent Living:	I plan to live with my parents while going to a community college for two years and then live in a dorm at the university. Eventually, I want to get married and have a house of my own.

Course of Study

Year 1 Age 14/15	Year 2 Age 15/16	Year 3 Age 16/17	Year 4 Age 17/18
Math I	Math II	Math III	First Aid/CPR
English I	English II	English III	English IV
World History	P.E.	American History	Govt./Free Enterprise
Biology	Earth Science	Early Childhood Development	Psychology
Keyboarding/Health	Culinary Arts I/II	Culinary Arts III/IV	Comm. Based Empl.
Career Exploration	Human Services	TA in kinder classroom	Comm. Based Empl.

49

For a student with a more moderate disability, an example of the desired postsecondary outcomes and the resulting course of study might look like this:

Postschool Outcome/Vision

Employment:	I would like to work around people and animals.
Community Participation:	I like sports and participating in the Special Olympics Program. I attend a singing group at church and sing in choir.
Recreation & Leisure:	I will continue to be active in Special Olympics and church activities. I am looking into participating in a bowling league. I like to fish and camp and will continue these outdoor activities. I also watch TV.
Postsecondary Training & Learning Opportunities:	I would like to work full-time after graduation so any training will be on the job.
Independent Living:	I will be capable of living with a friend or roommate but will need assistance with budgeting, buying food, and paying monthly bills.

Course of Study

Year 1 Age 14/15	Year 2 Age 15/16	Year 3 Age 16/17	Year 4 Age 17/18
LS (Life Skills) Math	LS Math	LS Math—money management	LS Math—purchasing and budgeting
LS Language Arts	LS Language Arts	LS Language Arts	LS Language Arts
Social Living	Social Living	Portfolio Development	Portfolio Development
Employment Skills	Community Based Instruction	Work Experience	Work Experience
Community Training	Portfolio Development	Culinary Arts	P.E.
P.E.	P.E.	Daily Living Skills	Daily Living Skills
Art for Enjoyment	Community Based Assessment	P.E.	Independent Living
	Culinary Arts	Social Living	Social Living

Source: O'Leary & Collision (2002), Mountain Plains Regional Resource Center, by permission.

Many employment-related transition goals or work readiness goals can be addressed in classroom-based career-vocational education programs or through structured work experiences in jobs within the school.

For example, in a computer skills class, students might search online for information about entry qualifications or certification requirements for licensure in specific technical careers. They might work several hours a week in the main office or library, or setting up equipment in the science labs. Specific skills such as answering telephones, typing, or computer work could be practiced. While on the job, student-worker behaviors such as punctuality, organization, working under supervision, relationships with co-workers and with authority, and staying on task could be observed, developed, and evaluated. Working in the cafeteria, for example, could provide students with concrete application of food preparation skills. Selling tickets at a school event or working in the school store provides similar opportunities to apply money management skills.

The development of personal and social skills can be addressed in classes and school activities that promote student interaction, particularly with nondisabled peers. To strengthen skills in the social domain, the students could work in a team with peers to plan a school social event or work on an aspect of the school newsletter or yearbook. They might join the school play or chorus. In connection with a school leadership club, they might participate in a student study group to explore how to improve social relationships among students or develop school pride. Under the independent living domain, many functional or daily living skills can be addressed in classes the school typically offers. Examples include the following:

- Food purchase and preparation in home economics or math class, or in the school cafeteria or store;
- Money management in math class;
- Reading survival words, using the phone book, reading the help wanted ads, movie schedule, or bus schedule in English class;
- Personal hygiene awareness in health or home economics class;
- Driving or transportation skills in driver's education class.

Recreational and leisure skills could be developed in physical education classes and in sports such as swimming, baseball, or basketball. Nonacademic courses such as music, art, dance, creative writing, or home economics offer students opportunities to develop appreciation for ways to use leisure time constructively. After-school clubs such as astronomy, chorus, drama, and band offer opportunities for growth and social involvement. Linkages with community recreation programs and youth-related programs (e.g., Boys and Girls Clubs) also help students integrate physical activity into their lives and develop social relationships.

There are many creative ways that transition goals, in a spectrum of domains, can be achieved using the resources and natural activities and events within the school. Seeking these in-school opportunities may be crucial in rural and remote areas where there may be limited opportuni-

51

ties to participate and practice skills in community-based employment settings (National Information Center for Children and Youth with Disabilities [NICHCY], 2003).

Case Illustrations for a Coordinated Set of Activities

The planning process for a coordinated set of activities includes:

1. Plan for transition from middle to high school (age 14).
2. Establish the long-range postsecondary goal.
3. Write the coordinated set of activities, including academic curriculum and course of study, career/occupational curriculum decisions, and options.
4. Identify related and supportive services.
5. Identify appropriate community-based support services and participating agencies.

The following sections illustrate how a "coordinated set of activities" can be implemented for students at different ages.

Sample Postschool Goals: Eric, Age 14

Student: Eric is a 14-year-old eighth-grade student with developmental disabilities.

Present Levels of Performance. Eric is a 14-year-old who is part of the middle school inclusion program. He is entering the ninth grade next school year. His academic classes are co-taught by general and special education teachers. In nonacademic activities, such as chorus, Eric participates without direct special education staff support. It is possible that Eric may be able to achieve a general education diploma. Eric is reading at the fourth-grade level and has not met proficiency in the state mathematics assessment. He participated in a career assessment at age 13 and expressed an interest in computer classes and music. He is uncertain what careers would be available to him, but he is vocal in his dislikes for certain careers such as cooking or maintenance. Eric learns best through a hands-on approach.

1. **Establish Postschool Goals.**

   Postschool employment goal: Eric and his parents have not yet identified any areas of career focus. He needs more exposure to the various career opportunities.

   Postschool goal for continuing education: Eric hopes to learn more about how music is made. His parents hope Eric can continue

52

to receive schooling after he graduates to improve his career options. **Community living goal:** Eric hopes to live on his own in the future near his parents. His parents want him to be prepared to live as independently as possible with supportive services available when he needs them. They expect that he will have a circle of friends.

2. **Write the Coordinated Set of Activities (academic, career-vocational, community-based learning experiences, and related services).**

   - *Instruction:* (1) Eric will be given the opportunity to participate in the ninth-grade curriculum with support from the Inclusion program. (2) Eric will be given the opportunity to participate in career exploration projects. (3) An initial career assessment will be conducted.

Sample Postschool Goals: Shawn, Age 15

Student: Shawn is a 15-year-old ninth-grade student with mental health and behavioral concerns.

1. **Establish the Long-Range Postschool Goals.**

   Postschool employment goal: Shawn plans to be employed while receiving support from the local mental health system. A career path will be determined through Shawn's participation in career assessment activities.

   Postschool goal for continuing education: Shawn has expressed the interest and desire to attend community college to learn about the music recording industry.

   Community living goal: After he graduates and gets a job, Shawn hopes to have his own apartment with friends and take care of his dog.

2. **Write the Coordinated Set of Activities (academic, career-vocational, community-based learning, and related services).** The coordinated set of activities may include any or all of the following areas.

   - *Instruction.* What classroom-based activities will be provided to the student to achieve the goals? (e.g., "Shawn will participate in the ninth-grade curriculum and will receive resource room support for reading three times a week").
   - *Related and community services.* What related and support services will help the student attain his or her stated goals? If the related and support services are listed in another section of the

IEP, then instead of repeating the information, simply reference that part of the document. For example, "Shawn's related services are listed in Part 3 of the IEP document." To meet student or family needs, what linkages to community services will the school provide? Example: "The school will provide Shawn and his parents with the names of agencies with mental health case coordination services and assist with a referral."

- *Community experiences.* What community-based instruction or learning experiences will be provided to the student? For example, "Shawn will be given the opportunity to participate in a 15-hour volunteer community service program."
- *Employment/postsecondary.* What activities will be performed by the school to assist the student in getting ready for the world of work or entering postsecondary education? For example, "The guidance counselor will work with Shawn to identify community colleges that offer a music production program and that offer counseling support services."
- *Functional life skill or activities of daily living.* What functional life skills will be addressed to assist the student in achieving the long term goals? For example, "With assistance of a behavioral specialist, Shawn will decrease disruptive behaviors in the classroom."
- *Functional vocational evaluation.* What informal or situational assessments will be performed to help the student identify career interests, preferences, and strengths? (e.g., "Shawn will receive a performance review at his current community service site to identify areas for growth and development in work skills.")

3. **Identify Appropriate Community Services and Participating Agencies.** None at this stage.

Sample Postschool Goals: Shawn, Age 16

Student: Shawn is now 16, has mental health and behavioral problems, and is two years from graduation.

Present Levels of Performance. Shawn is a 16-year-old young man who is academically below grade level in most subjects. Shawn has skills on the piano, specifically creating music background pieces and mixing sounds. He has expressed an interest in music recording and production. Shawn is inconsistent in his behavior toward peers and authority figures; his emotional difficulties have prevented him from being able to concentrate on his future or to make significant gains toward employment skills. Occasionally, when stressed, Shawn has become aggressive and destructive with property. He is learning to identify antecedent triggers to his aggressive outbursts. Shawn presently lives at home with his family. Shawn has learned to safely use public transportation and access public facilities for leisure/recreation.

1. **Establish Postschool Goals.**

   Employment: Shawn plans to be employed with supportive services from the mental health system. A career path will be determined by Shawn's participation in career assessment activities.

   Further Education: Shawn has expressed the interest and desire to go to community college someday to learn about the music production and recording industry.

   Community Living: After he graduates and gets a job, Shawn hopes to have his own apartment with friends and take care of his dog.

2. **Write the Coordinated Set of Activities (academic, career-vocational, community-based learning experiences, and related services).**

   - *Instruction:* Shawn will be offered the opportunity to work toward his eleventh-grade requirements in a supportive special education program combined with group counseling.
   - *Related and community services:* Shawn will receive counseling services through a joint program with the mental health agency. The school counselor will provide Shawn with the names of mental health agencies that provide services to support his needs in the postschool setting.
   - *Employment/postsecondary:* The school will provide Shawn the opportunity to take a career skills class to develop employment skills and behaviors. He will participate in the next level career assessment. Shawn will receive instruction in how to apply for part-time employment after school.
   - *Community experiences:* Shawn will participate in driver's education and the school counselor will provide Shawn with information to assist him to obtain a driver's license from the Department of Motor Vehicles. The school counselor will provide Shawn information about recreation opportunities in the community.

3. **Identify Appropriate Community Services and Participating Agencies.** *Example:* Career assessment, The Career Education division, James Clayburn, 534-995-XXXX. Group counseling, Mental Health Services, Marie Sanchez, 345-244-XXXX. (Adapted from O'Leary & Collision, 2002; New York State Department of Education, 2005).

Chapter 9

What Is the Role of Interagency Coordination in Transition?

In the past few decades, the successes and benefits of service coordination in health care, mental health services, and adult services have gained the attention of educators and policy makers. Since virtually all individuals with disabilities are being served by the public education system, there is a growing interest in developing interagency service coordination models for use within that system. There is also keen interest in linking community-based services with education to provide a comprehensive system of educational options for children, youths, adults, and their families.

A *systematic* approach to transition services means developing strategies to address the complex needs of youths with disabilities in an organized and coordinated manner to support multiple pathways to successful transition. Coordinated interagency service system is defined as a systematic, comprehensive, and coordinated system of secondary education and transition for individuals with disabilities that is provided in their communities in the most integrated settings possible, and in a manner that promotes individual choice and decision making. Interagency service coordination may also be defined as a strategy for mobilizing and organizing all of the appropriate resources to link the individual with needed services in order to achieve IEP goals and successful transition outcomes (Kochhar-Bryant, 2003).

System coordination at state, local, and school levels involves several functions, including *information and referral, identification and preparation, assessment and evaluation, IEP/transition planning and development, service coordination/linking, service monitoring and follow-along, individual and interagency advocacy, and service evaluation and follow-up* (Kochhar-Bryant, 2003; Research and Training Center on Service Coordination, 2001). Such an approach requires that schools reach out beyond their boundaries and seek a shared responsibility from the many agencies that provide services for students in transition.

How Can the Student Get Help from Non-School Agencies in the Last Year of High School?

IDEA 2004 requires school-linked human service agencies to support students' transition from school to postsecondary education and employment. A wide array of support services exists in local communities. By blending community supports and resources, transition programs can better assist students to achieve their postsecondary goals. Examples of such community services are provided in Table 9.1.

While the school system is required by law to provide the services that are written into the IEP, organizations that provide supportive services are expected to share the responsibility for transition support services. For example, if the student needs medical services, they can be sought and provided from Medicaid, public health agencies, private insurance, early periodic screening, diagnosis, and treatment programs. If transition support services are needed, they may be sought and provided from vocational rehabilitation agencies, employment services, adult service agencies, Job Training programs, Workforce Investment Act programs, or supported employment projects.

The student's IEP should contain a statement of interagency responsibilities or any linkages required to ensure that the student has the transition services needed from outside agencies and that representatives from those agencies are invited to attend IEP meetings. For example, if the IEP indicates that the student needs an assessment for vocational

TABLE 9.1. *Community Service Agencies That Support Students in Transition or Consult with IEP Teams*

• Developmental disabilities services	• Adult agencies
• Vocational rehabilitation services	• Advocacy organizations
• Community rehabilitation programs	• Assistive technology organizations
• Community or public health services	• Dropout prevention programs
• Community mental health services	• Business-education partnerships
• Residential or housing services	• Alcohol and substance abuse services
• Respite care services	• Correctional education or juvenile
• One-stop employment centers	services offices
• Postsecondary institutions (2- and 4-year colleges and technical training programs)	• Employers and employment specialists
	• Recreation and leisure programs
• Social work services	• Adult education programs
	• Parent training and information centers
	• Transportation offices

rehabilitation services by the VR agency, but that agency cannot provide such an assessment, then the local educational agency is required to reconvene the IEP team to identify alternative ways to meet the transition objectives. The transition coordinator must invite representatives from those agencies to attend the meetings.

This requirement for interagency collaboration and shared responsibility means that (a) schools must develop a seamless system of supports to assist the student to make a successful transition to postsecondary life, (b) the student and family must be engaged in transition planning well before graduation, and (c) there must be formal interagency agreements between schools and cooperating agencies. Studies of best practices indicate that effective transition requires structured interagency coordination, such as interagency agreements or memoranda of understanding (MOUs) among agencies (Lueking & Certo, 2002; NCSET, 2004, 2002). Both IDEA and NCLB encourage strategic partnerships and structured agreements among schools and community service agencies.

Need to Improve Interagency Linkages

Despite federal mandates, more work needs to be done to create smooth transitions for youths (Hart, Zimbrich, & Whelley, 2002). For example, teachers responding to a national survey by the U.S. Department of Education reported that, in the area of youth transition, more than half rarely, if ever, coordinate referrals to adult service providers (Study of Personnel Needs in Special Education [SPeNSE], 2002). Data from the National Longitudinal Transition Study (Wagner, Newman, Cameto, & Levine, 2005) show that more than 85 percent of secondary special education students were unable to receive services from community agencies until after high school. These conditions exist despite the IDEA requirement that a student's IEP include a statement of interagency responsibilities or any needed linkages, if appropriate, to ensure that youths will receive the services needed to achieve their postsecondary education or career goals.

All states are taking some action to provide direction and resources for improving linkages between schools and service providers. Ten states reported that they have passed legislation or regulations specifically providing for greater coordination between schools and services providers. In addition, while less than half of school districts reported having a transition coordinator at each high school, all but three states reported hiring state transition coordinators who can assist teachers in their efforts to link students with providers after high school. All states reported providing technical assistance to local educational agencies on interagency coordination (General Accounting Office, 2003).

How Is an Interagency Agreement Developed?

School districts are not expected to work alone in developing and delivering transition services. As required under IDEA 2004, school districts are encouraged to coordinate with other service systems and formalize relationships that can be called upon for advice, provision of services, and resources. This section summarizes strategies to establish relationships with agencies and participate in interagency planning groups on transition. Each community defines its interagency mission differently, so no two interagency agreements will look alike. However, though they may look different in each service system, there is a basic blueprint for crafting an effective agreement to accomplish common goals within specific time periods.

The Mission Statement

The **mission statement** should describe the broad purpose of the transition interagency agreement and the areas of joint responsibility. The statement generally describes what each cooperating partner will contribute toward the goal of transition service delivery and improvement and may describe what the partnership is not designed to do. A mission statement generally includes all or several of the following four parts:

1. *A statement of context or history.* This is usually a brief introductory paragraph that broadly describes the interagency partnership; how it was initiated; how it addresses current transition needs; how it improves upon current transition practices; and how the partnership may differ from, or expand, what has been in place before.
2. *A statement of the authority for the interagency agreement.* This introductory section of the mission statement refers to the legal basis for the agreement and may list local, state, and federal laws, regulations, or policies that give authority to this agreement.
3. *General statement of purpose of the agreement and expected outcomes.* This includes a broad statement of what the partnership expects to accomplish and what results it hopes to see for youths in transition.
4. *The broad goal and outline of roles and responsibilities.* Describes what the agreement provides and the roles and responsibilities of each cooperating partner.

A mission statement is a broad description or the *vision* of the interagency partnership, not a specific set of goals and objectives. Mission statements generally serve as a preamble to a cooperative agreement that defines goals and objectives for the partnership.

The Cooperative Agreement

Once the mission statement is completed, the next step is to decide among collaborating agencies the specific agreements for action to achieve the mission. The *cooperative agreement,* or *memorandum of understanding (MOU),* incorporates the mission statement and provides more detail about the commitments of the agencies involved. Useful questions to consider are:

- How does the team develop such a cooperative agreement to meet specific annual goals?
- How can goal statements be crafted in such a way that the team can measure the results of the interagency coordination activities?
- How does the team develop a timetable for action?

The cooperative agreement is essential to the development of effective interagency coordination for it defines the structure, processes, and local authority for action among the collaborating agencies. It also defines what can be expected from each agency—their activities, responsibilities, and contributions to the transition service delivery system. Cooperative agreements accomplish four things: (1) identify resources to support the interagency relationship; (2) identify goals, objectives, and activities of cooperating agencies; (3) identify expected results of the interagency partnership; and (4) establish timetables for the activities.

Resources. Cooperative agreements broadly outline the particular contribution from each cooperating agency and the length of time it will commit. More comprehensive cooperative agreements specify the resources that will be provided by each agency, including staff, funds, equipment, consultation time, vehicles, space, and other resources. Plans to transfer, redistribute, or match these resources are also described.

Goals, Objectives and Activities. The cooperative agreement describes the goals, objectives, and activities to be performed by the cooperating agencies. The agreements should also describe the role and authority of the interagency coordinator and interagency planning team.

Expected Results (Outcomes). This section defines the expected results or outcomes for students and families involved in transition services and for the cooperating agencies. Examples of outcomes include the following:

- Increased participation in community-based work experiences;
- Greater percentage of students with disabilities who receive the general education diploma;

60

- Increased enrollment of students with disabilities in two- and four-year colleges;
- Increased rate of entry into employment after graduation;
- Greater percentage of students living independently;
- Greater percentage of seniors who access needed adult services.

Methods to evaluate results should be described along with the roles of cooperating agencies, students, and families in the evaluation process. The agreement should also clearly describe the interagency planning team's authority for evaluating and monitoring the coordination activities.

Timetable.   The agreement should include the date the interagency relationship takes effect, the schedule for accomplishing objectives, and the dates for reviewing and modifying the agreement.

Involving Agencies in the IEP Process

Interagency cooperative agreements identify the roles and responsibilities of each agency involved with a particular student. How are outside agencies involved in the transition IEP process? As part of the process of inviting non-school agencies to participate in the IEP planning process, the IEP team follows a set of procedures.

Before contacting any outside community agency, the school discusses the range of community services with the student and his or her family in order to reach agreement about which agencies are most appropriate to invite to the IEP meeting. This needs to be done well before the IEP meeting is scheduled. The school then obtains a consent for release of information from the parent (or from the student if he or she has reached age of majority and is his or her own legal guardian) in order to contact the community agency and discuss its involvement in the student's IEP meeting. IDEA 2004 outlines procedures for the transfer of parental rights to the student when he or she reaches the age of majority under state law. These agreements should be included in the IEP document, with a signature of the agency representative.

What Is the Role of the Local Interagency Transition Planning Council?

An interagency transition planning council is one strategy to increase the availability, access, and quality of transition services in the school or district. The local transition planning council may have different names in different communities, including "community transition team," "interagency community council," "interagency planning team," or "local transition advisory group." The planning council may be purely advisory, or have decision-making authority. As a decision-making body, the council may decide on the direction and operation of the interagency partnership, its goals and objectives, its management and staff, the use of resources, distribution of resources, and target populations.

The functions of a transition planning council typically include (1) coordination of services to ensure non-duplication and cost-effectiveness; (2) sharing responsibility for assisting students and families to link with community services; (3) providing a quality, local service delivery system to support transition; (4) anticipating current and future needs for services and developing plans to build capacity to meet those needs; (5) improving student outcomes in adult living, learning, and employment roles; (6) developing a registry of adult service agency representatives who can attend IEP/transition planning meetings and act as resources to the transition process; and (7) developing formal interagency agreements in which information about eligibility can be shared, needs assessed, gaps in services identified, and service capacity strengthened.

Developing the Local Advisory Council Team

The local advisory council should include a relatively small group of concerned, knowledgeable, and committed individuals. A small group is often more effective in directing and monitoring interagency coordination than a large assembly. The local council should include a balance in representation among school and community agencies, individuals with disabilities, and parent representatives. Local councils typically include representatives from special education, general education, career-technical education, two- and four-year colleges, vocational-technical training institutions, adults with disabilities (particularly those who have received transition services), parents of youths with disabilities, local business or industry, vocational rehabilitation services, community service agencies, adult service providers, and additional public and private service providers.

A council chair should be designated to serve as the lead interagency coordinator or liaison. A long-range plan of two to five years should be developed to sustain the program. The council should define short- and long-range goals within an established timetable, assess the transition needs of youths in the system, and define expected outcomes or impacts on youths and families. It is important that the council have the authority to determine the direction of the interagency partnership and review its accomplishments on a regular basis.

Getting Started in the Community

To find out if your community has a transition team and how you can get involved, contact your school district's special education department or office of student service. Ask who directs transition services for students with disabilities in the district. You may also contact the local Parent Training and Information Center (PTI) at the state or local level, or the regional special education resource center. If a local transition team does not exist in your community, then collaborate with others to create one. The following steps may be useful:

1. *Do your homework.* Explore what your community is already doing to provide transition services to youths. Explore the range of transition services being provided in your school and community by talking with school professionals, student, parents, and community and parent groups, or search district and state websites.
2. *Identify areas that need improvement.* Decide what transition services are the highest priority and which of the service gaps you want to address. Talk with others to gain some consensus on the priorities for action. Locate any available needs assessments, special education improvement reports, parent or student satisfaction summaries, and similar documents that might address transition needs.
3. *Create an action plan.* Talk with school professionals, parents, community and parent groups, and others about strategies to address these service gaps. Share your assessment information with others and enlist them to examine transition services in other districts. Create an inquiry group to conduct research.
4. *Evaluate your plan.* Define how you will measure the success of your efforts. What results or outcomes are you expecting and how will you know when you have achieved them? Agree on what measures you will use to determine if your efforts are successful (adapted from NICHCY, 2002).

Using Interagency Evaluation Information to Improve Transition Services

Local transition teams can be a powerful force within the community for systemic change and improvement of services to youths. A collaborative interagency team can see the system as a whole and can make strategic decisions about what resources are needed to improve services and what services best match the assessed needs of youths in the community. Evaluation is an important tool in this process. It involves acting upon evaluation data collected from the multiple sources and agencies to improve the transition service system. Such improvement requires a constructive process for:

1. Analyzing and communicating the information in a manner that is understandable and usable by different stakeholder groups (e.g., service coordinators, students/families, administrators); and,
2. Systematically using the information to make changes and improvements in the service system to ensure that services match the assessed needs of youths and families.

Armed with valuable evaluation information, transition councils can promote actions through school boards and other governmental entities in areas such as policy and funding. Table 9.2 presents features of effective interagency agreements.

TABLE 9.2   *Essential Features of Effective Interagency Agreements*

- Responsibility for design, revision, and implementation of the agreement shared by participating agency staff
- Commitment in the development and implementation of the agreement shared by participating agency directors
- Input from direct service staff in the design, revision, and implementation of the agreement
- Regular opportunities to meet, discuss ideas, and develop relationships
- Willingness of agencies to learn from each other and see how each can benefit from the mission of the other organizations
- Active involvement in strategic planning by participating agency representatives
- Utilization of data to determine the impact and outcomes resulting from the agreement
- Utilization of data for strategic planning and continuous improvement
- Dissemination of the agreement to direct service practitioners
- Technical assistance provided to direct service practitioners regarding implementation of the agreement (Crane, Gramlich, & Peterson, 2004).

Table 9.3 summarizes beginning steps that can be taken by students, families and professionals to establish or strengthen a transition program where one does not exist.

TABLE 9.3 *Getting Started with Transition*

Student	• Write down your long-term goals and what you think you need to do to reach them. • Read your IEP and transition plan and decide if the plan is being implemented. • Tell your teachers you want to lead your own IEP meeting and ask them to help you learn what to do. • Learn about your civil rights under the law, such as IDEA and the Americans with Disabilities Act. • Learn about your disability, how to explain to people your strengths, and how to ask for reasonable accommodations. • Practice job interviews and asking for accommodations. • Talk with your doctor and parents about your health care needs so you will be ready to take responsibility for them. • Ask your teacher how to get involved with your community's transition team.
Family Members	• Observe your son's or daughter's independent living skills, work behaviors, social involvement, dreams, and hopes. • Call your child's teachers and ask that transition services, including financial planning, be addressed at your next meeting. • Help your child learn about his or her disability and how to ask for the supports he or she needs. • Give your child responsibility for chores at home. • Role play different situations with your child (e.g., interviews). • Discuss your child's medical needs with him or her and facilitate discussions with your doctor. • Introduce your child to adult role models with disabilities. • Look in your phone book and Yellow Pages and identify three new possible resources to help your son's or daughter's transition to adult activities.
School or Agency Administrators	• Evaluate transition services in your system. • Look into establishing or strengthening your community transition team. • Develop a new community agency contact. • Find some funding to share across agencies or for service development. • Set up a meeting with staff members to learn each person's expertise in transition. • Develop a cooperative agreement with another agency specifying how to coordinate transition. • Encourage your staff to be creative in problem solving.
Special Educators	• Talk to students and families about transition services. • Ask to attend a conference, workshop, or other learning opportunity related to transition. • Teach students about their civil rights under the law, such as the Americans with Disabilities Act. • Pledge to conduct collaborative, needs-based IEP meetings that empower youth and families.

(continued)

TABLE 9.3 *Continued*

Special Educators (*continued*)	• Provide youth with step-by-step activities that familiarize them with the IEP process and prepare them to take active roles. • Call the local rehabilitation counselor or mental retardation case manager and coordinate a meeting.
Vocational Educators	• Contact a special educator and find out when IEPs are scheduled for your current or future students. • Offer to provide a tour of your program and share your knowledge and expertise in job competencies, job development, and job placement. • Identify one student receiving special education services and work with him or her to provide vocational counseling to help define realistic career goals. • Develop a plan to coordinate your work-study program with all the special education community-based work programs.
Guidance Counselors	• Create a workshop for students on self-advocacy skills that would promote success in postsecondary education or employment settings. • Ask to attend a workshop, inservice, or other training to learn about community agencies and resources. • Ask a college representative about services for students with disabilities.
Community Service Agency Providers	• Attend a workshop, inservice, or other training to learn about community agencies and resources. • Develop a folder that contains some of the wealth of information you have about community resources and how to access them, and share with IEP team members, transition councils, families, students, and administrators. • Identify three things that could help you actively participate in the IEP process when appropriate and share these with the high school administrator or special educator/transition specialist.
Vocational Rehabilitation Counselors	• Schedule regular office hours in schools. • Support activities and use of assistive technology for students in high school that result in employment. • Serve on a local transition committee. • Share your knowledge of the job market and job assessments.

Source: NICHY, 2002.

Chapter 10

How Can Transition and Standards-Based Education Be Blended?

Educators are grappling with many complex questions as they attempt to comply with the mandate to improve access to the general education curriculum for students with disabilities (Center on Education Policy, 2003). The challenge to expand transition services has become even more complex as general education reforms place increasing emphasis on academic performance for students and less emphasis on career-vocational development and community-based learning. Standards-based educational systems with high-stakes testing present challenges to both the individualized education and individualized transition planning models required by IDEA. Creative new approaches to blending the standards-based and individualized education approaches are being sought. This chapter compares the principles and assumptions that undergird both transition services and standards-based education, discusses challenges to aligning the two educational models, and discusses transition as a unifying framework for creating bridges between them.

How can the standards-based curriculum be reconciled or aligned with the individualized education process? How should students with disabilities be included in standardized assessments? The standards-based educational model is grounded in the assumption that all students should meet common standards for what should be taught and learned. However, the individualized education process is grounded in the principle of "appropriate" education that meets individual needs of each student who needs specialized educational services. The standards-based system and individualized system must be aligned to support students who need special education services. As a result, professional collaboration to align these systems has taken center stage in IDEA 2004 and NCLB.

How Do NCLB and IDEA Differ in Principles and Policies?

In considering the twin goals of *equity* (access for all) and *excellence* (high standards) in education, it is important to understand the differences between the principles that underlie NCLB and IDEA. For more than two decades, the primary policy tool for improving outcomes for students with disabilities has been the Individuals with Disabilities Education Act and its provisions for free and appropriate education and protection of individual rights. Standards-based education under NCLB has introduced a fundamentally different set of policies and practices that are based on uniform learning standards within a *standards-based curriculum.* The students' mastery of the curriculum content is measured by standardized tests or assessments. Standards-based education (SBE) is based on the assumption that *common standards for all students* are a catalyst for improved educational results and serve as a basis for what should be taught and for measuring what students should be expected to know (Kochhar-Bryant & Bassett, 2003; McDonnell, McLaughlin, & Morison, 1997). SBE is also based on the assumptions that (a) content and performance standards can be clearly and precisely defined, (b) student performance can be measured validly and reliably, and (c) accountability can be strengthened through public reporting of aggregate data on student performance.

In contrast to the assumption of common performance standards, special education services are guided by the special education framework, which defines the rights of students with disabilities to a free and appropriate education and specifies the responsibilities of school systems to accommodate their individual needs (McDonnel, McLaughlin, & Morison, 1997). Individualized education relies on a *private process—* the IEP and transition plans are centered on the *needs of the individual student,* and *students' individual rights* are enforced through a set of procedural safeguards. Also, in contrast to the focus on academic outcomes that are the hallmark of standards-based education, the special education framework for students with disabilities encompasses a broader range of educational outcomes for students with disabilities.

Also, in contrast to the focus on academic outcomes that are the hallmark of standards-based education, the transition service framework for students with disabilities includes a broad range of educational outcomes for students with disabilities. For example, Ysseldyke and his colleagues clustered outcomes into eight domains, including presence and participation, accommodation and adaptation, physical health, responsibility and independence, contribution and citizenship, academic and functional literacy, personal and social adjustment, and satisfaction (Ysseldyke, Olsen, & Thurlow, 1997; Ysseldyke, Thurlow, Langenfeld, Nelson, Teelucksing, & Seyfurth, 1998). Critics of standards-based education for all students claim that states have crafted standards that are too narrow and do not allow for educators to include nonacademic learning objectives such as those that are focused on social and behavioral skills, career and vocational development, physical and health development, and functional skills (Izzo, Hertzfeld, Simmons-Reed, & Aaron, 2001; Kochhar-Bryant & Bassett, 2003). To address the broader life domains of the student, the foundation for transition must be laid during the elementary and middle school years, guided by the broad concept of career development and preparation of the whole person for postsecondary life (Sitlington & Clark, 2006). Table 10.1 compares the assumptions of individualized (IDEA) and standards-based (NCLB) education.

IDEA 1997 and 2004 emphasized the importance of an equitable accountability system and required states to include students with disabilities in general state- and district-wide assessments and school improvement efforts. States are now required to establish goals for the performance of children with disabilities and assess their progress toward achieving those goals. They must establish indicators such as student participation in assessments, dropout rates, graduation rates, and guidelines for alternate assessment of children with disabilities. However, *IDEA also protects the child's right to "appropriate" and "individualized" methods for achieving common standards and goals, including nonacademic goals.* The challenge for educators is to align standards-based education policies with those under IDEA that are based on individual rights and individualized educational processes. Transition, therefore, must be viewed as a comprehensive framework (a) to ensure

TABLE 10.1. *Comparing the Assumptions of Individualized Education and Standards-Based Education*

Transition under IDEA	Standards-Based Education
• Emphasizes a range of educational outcomes	• Focus on academic and basic literacy outcomes
• Is an individualized process	• Emphasizes common rigorous learning standards for all students
• Curriculum matches the student's postschool goals	• Performance can be measured validly and reliably through testing
• Emphasizes a career-oriented curriculum for student not bound for postsecondary education	• Decreases "low-track" English, math, science classes
• Involves interagency coordination and support	• Increases enrollment in college prep courses
• Improves transition outcomes	• Greater inclusion in general education
	• Improves transition outcomes

Source: Kochhar-Bryant, C., & Bassett, D. (2003). *Aligning Transition and Standards-Based Education.* Columbus, OH: Merrill/Prentice Hall.

effective alignment between secondary education and transition services, and (b) to guide planning and decision making among students, families, and professionals.

How Does Transition "Fit" with Standards-Based Education?

Efforts to implement the federal transition requirements have been fraught with uncertainty about what is expected of states and local educational agencies, families, and students. As a result, progress in implementing transition in many states has not resulted in significant improvement in postsecondary outcomes for youths. Many educators have called for a unified vision of middle and secondary education and transition planning (Clark, Sitlington, & Kolstoe, 2000; National Council on Disability, 2000; Thompson, Fulk, & Piercy, 2000). New questions have arisen about the relationship between transition and standards-based education.

- Is transition supposed to "fit" into the standards-based reform movement, or do standards-based educational practices fit within the broader career development and transition framework for students with disabilities?
- To what extent do schools have the responsibility for preparing youths for careers if they are not bound for postsecondary education after graduation?
- How can "transition" be implemented for students who are in inclusive middle or secondary classrooms?

Until recently, the concept of "transition" has implied a separate postschool planning process in which students with disabilities work with special educators to develop transition plans, while students without disabilities work with guidance counselors to develop graduation plans. The perception of transition as a separate planning process makes it difficult to integrate needed transition services when students are participating in the general education curriculum. Transition planning should not be viewed as conflicting with participation in the general education curriculum or meeting high academic standards and graduating with a regular high school diploma.

Students who need transition services should not be forced to choose between transition services and the general education curriculum. The potential benefits of aligning transition and standards-based (general) educational systems are enormous. First, transition research has demonstrated that students in successful transition and school-to-work programs are highly integrated with their nondisabled peers in both school and

70

community activities. Second, transition personnel are now more likely to be teachers, counselors, or coordinators who serve both students with and without disabilities. Third, the IDEA and NCLB transition requirements emphasize transition practices that maximize students' integration with nondisabled peers. A core principle for secondary students with disabilities is that the IEPs must reflect the general education curriculum and standards, participation in standardized assessments, and needed transition services. Misperceptions about the relationship of transition planning to the general education curriculum illustrates the tensions that arise between the goals of individualized educational planning and the standards-based education model (common standards for all). As one parent put it, "I don't want to have to choose between general education advantages *or* transition services. My son should have both" (10/10/05, personal communication).

Transition as a Unifying Framework

Implementation of transition programs within a standards-based education framework presents a conceptual and practical challenge for educators, many who see the principles and goals as mutually exclusive. This section discusses issues and barriers to bridging standards-based education and transition. To align special education programs with general education reforms and improve postsecondary outcomes, IDEA 1997 and 2004 added new requirements that were designed to ensure that youths have greater access to the secondary education curriculum and standardized assessments. IDEA *emphasized both transition services and access to the general education curriculum. This emphasis, therefore, placed expectations on state and local educational agencies to seek practical solutions for aligning secondary education and transition systems.* The requirement logically holds educational agencies responsible for providing appropriate transition planning through the IEP, secondary education curriculum accommodations and redesign, and interagency coordination to help students and families achieve postsecondary goals.

Experts agree that, while challenging, many school districts across the United States are designing education that is based on both common standards and the right of students with disabilities to an individualized education and transition planning. The transition planning framework can be instrumental as a comprehensive, foundational framework for:

1. Incorporating the concept of integrated transition planning and participation in a general education course of study;
2. Recognizing different pathways to graduation for different students;
3. Guiding decision making among students, families, and profession-

als for postsecondary planning;

4. Meeting universal design (UDL) criteria of flexible and widely usable curricula and environments;
5. Recognizing the need for flexible combinations of academic, career-vocational classes, and community-based work experiences to achieve different pathways to graduation.

Building on traditional career development frameworks, Kohler (1998) characterized the high school years as requiring a "transition perspective" for education of youths with disabilities. Kochhar-Bryant and Bassett (2003) referred to transition as a "unifying framework" for aligning standards-based education and transition services (see Figure 10.1). Transition planning, therefore, is the foundational concept and integrates the four building blocks of individualized education—curriculum standards, outcomes in multiple life domains, opportunities to learn

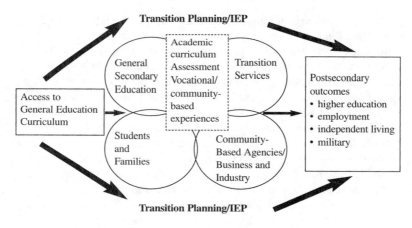

FIGURE 10.1 *Transition as a Unifying Framework*

Source: Kochhar-Bryant, C., & Bassett, D. (2003). *Aligning Transition and Standards-Based Education.* Columbus, OH: Merrill/Prentice Hall.

(accommodations and supports) (Glatthorn and Craft-Tripp, 2000), and curriculum choices.

"Opportunity standards" are an important element in a framework for aligning standards-based education and the provision of individualized and appropriate transition planning. Glatthorn & Craft-Tripp (2000) synthesized the various "opportunities" that a local school needs to provide for helping students achieve the performance standards now required of all students. Examples of opportunities that are needed by students with disabilities to participate in the general education classroom include the following:

- A planned program of study built around postsecondary transition goals;
- Individualized educational program;
- Individualized instruction;
- Grouping that does not stigmatize students;
- A responsive curriculum;
- Adequate time for learning;
- Extended school year programming;
- Positive behavioral interventions;
- Responsiveness to native language;
- Valid assessment.

Glatthorn and Craft-Tripp (2000) concluded that setting educational goals for many students with disabilities means looking beyond academic goals to a broader set of outcomes. As others have previously suggested (Halpern, 1994; Patton & Dunn, 1998; Polloway et al., 1991; Tashie, Shapiro-Barnard, Dillon, Schuh, & Jorgenson, 2001), a focus on a broad set of outcomes means that curricula for some students with disabilities, particularly at the secondary level, include nonacademic components and emphasis on the transition to work and other aspects of adult life.

Blending Multiple Standards

Transition planning to achieve postsecondary goals includes a variety of standards: (1) academic curriculum standards, (2) occupational skill standards, and (3) opportunity standards to assist students to progress in their educational programs (supports and accommodations). Transition planning, the foundational concept, integrates the four building blocks of individualized education—standards, outcomes in multiple domains, opportunities, and curriculum options (Figure 10.2).

In summary, a transition planning process that blends standards and opportunities:

- Is a process of continuous, systematic planning, coordination, and decision making to define and achieve postsecondary goals;
- Provides curriculum options or pathways to accommodate student's needs and different postsecondary goals;
- Blends academic, career-technical, and community-based learning;
- Addresses multiple outcome domains and measures; and
- Integrates appropriate aids and supports (opportunities).

73

Transition planning provides the passage or "bridge" between school and adult life for students with disabilities.

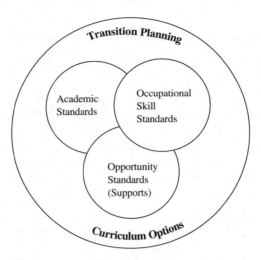

FIGURE 10.2 *Blending Multiple Standards*

Chapter 11

What Is the New Summary of Performance under IDEA 2004?

The Legal Mandate: Section 504 and the ADA

In 2002, the U.S. Department of Justice and the U.S. Department of Education clarified that schools were not required to conduct evaluations on students leaving high school. The Office for Civil Rights (OCR) stated that "neither your high school nor your postsecondary school is required to conduct or pay for a new evaluation to document your disability and need for an academic adjustment" (U.S. Office of Civil Rights, 2002, p. 3). Under this policy, the student is the only one responsible for gathering and paying for disability documentation evaluation. Advocates for youths with disabilities observe that this change has the potential to significantly limit access to postsecondary supports and accommodations. Consumers who could not afford to pay several thousand dollars for a psychoeducational evaluation could be denied access to protections under Section 504 and the ADA in postsecondary settings (Shaw, 2005). This would particularly affect the outcomes for students with very limited fiscal resources.

Changes in Diagnostic Information Required of Secondary Schools

IDEA 2004 has dramatically changed the diagnostic information that secondary schools are required to develop for students. First, in Section 300.307 it specifies that the discrepancy model (i.e., the difference between academic performance and ability as measured by a psychoeducational evaluation) may not be the only approach used to identify students with learning disabilities (LD). The proposed alternative to the discrepancy model is the use of scientific, research-based interventions (Sec. 300.309(a)(2)(i)). This is consistent with the law's focus on prevention as the key to limit overidentification of students with LD. The primary prevention approach that has been recommended in the literature is *Response to Intervention* (RTI). Although RTI has been identified in the special education research literature as an effective early intervention model, it has not been validated for the purpose of identification and documentation of students with learning disabilities (Kavale, Holdnack, & Mostert, 2005). It is likely, however, that over the next few years there will be increasing numbers of students identified as LD using RTI with reduced reliance on psychoeducational evaluations (Kovaleski & Prasse, 2004; National Joint Committee on Learning Disabilities, 2005).

Previously, schools understood that students typically needed a comprehensive reevaluation every three years. Now IEP teams need only consider whether and what kind of additional diagnostic information is needed. The new regulations specify that a reevaluation "must occur at least once every 3 years, unless the parent and the public agency agree that a reevaluation is unnecessary" (Sec. 300. 303(b)(2)). It is, therefore, possible in coming years that some students with disabilities could leave high school without having been "formally" tested since middle school or even elementary school. Although this policy makes sense in that automatically retesting all students every three years until they leave high school is not a necessary or productive use of skilled personnel, it does have serious implications for achieving postsecondary goals. The most critical policy change, however, relates to evaluation of students exiting high school.

IDEA 2004 indicates that a comprehensive evaluation "shall not be required before the termination of a child's eligibility under this part due to graduation from secondary school with a regular diploma, or due to exceeding the age eligibility for a free appropriate public education under State law" (IDEA, 2004, Sec. 300.305(e)(2)). It calls instead for a *Summary of Performance* (SOP), which specifies that "a local educational agency shall provide the child with a summary of the child's academic achievement and functional performance, which shall include recommendations on how to assist the child in meeting the child's postsecondary goals" (IDEA, 2004, Sec. 300.305(e)(3)).

Strengthening the Bridge: Why a Summary of Performance?

In elementary and secondary school, teachers and other school professionals share the responsibility for the educational success with the student, but *in higher education and work settings it is up to the individual.* Students must have the skills to advocate for their needs in college or on the job. An SOP that provides documentation of the disability, summary of the student's academic achievement and functional performance, and recommendations on how to help the student meet his or her postsecondary goals (IDEA, 2004, Sec. 614) can help bridge the gap for students exiting from high school. Since IDEA did not provide specific guidance to states on how the SOP should be structured, great flexibility is allowed.

The Summary of Performance, with the accompanying documentation, is important to assist the student as he or she makes the transition from high school to postsecondary education or employment. This information is necessary under Section 504 of the Rehabilitation Act and the Americans with Disabilities Act to help establish a student's eligibility for reasonable accommodations and supports in *postsecondary* settings. It is also helpful in the Vocational Rehabilitation Comprehensive Assessment process to determine eligibility for VR services. The information about students' current level of functioning is intended to help postsecondary institutions consider accommodations for access. *The recommendations in an SOP should not imply that any individual who qualified for special education in high school will automatically qualify for the same services in the postsecondary education or the employment setting.* Postsecondary institutions and employers will continue to make eligibility decisions on a case-by-case basis.

Goal of the SOP

The goal of the Summary of Performance is to enhance post-high school outcomes for students with disabilities by providing them with relevant information about their academic achievement and functional performance. It is meant to be a useful step to help students with disabilities to improve access to postsecondary education and employment. The Summary of Performance is intended to describe students' current performance and functional limitations based on a historical review of assessments and services (Shaw, 2005). It should identify accommodations and supports that were effective in high school that may have utility in postschool settings. Furthermore, under Section 504 of the Rehabilitation Act and the Americans with Disabilities Act (ADA) employers and postsecondary institutions need to obtain information to document a disability, determine the current impact of the disability, and justify the need for accommodations (Shaw, 2005). Given the importance of this requirement to students and postsecondary personnel, professionals who work with students with disabilities at the secondary level need to know what information to include in the SOP. Unfortunately, the procedures necessary to produce this summary of the student's achievement and functional performance were not made clear by the IDEA regulations.

Structure and Development of the SOP

National Transition Documentation Summit

To meet the policy challenge presented by IDEA 2004, a group of professionals known as the National Transition Documentation Summit worked for almost two years to develop an effective Summary of Performance that would meet the needs of secondary and postsecondary personnel as well as consumers (i.e., parents and students). Representatives from several national organizations worked collaboratively to develop a model SOP that would meet the transition needs of students with disabilities by bridging the gap between IDEA and 504/ADA. These organizations included the Council for Exceptional Children's Division on Career Development and Transition (DCDT) and Division on Learning Disabilities (DLD), the National Center on Learning Disabilities (NCLD), Learning Disability Association (LDA), the National Joint Committee on Learning Disabilities (NJCLD), and the National Association of School Psychologists (NASP). Electronic communication, along with face-to-face meetings at the Association on Higher Education and Disability conference in the summer of 2004 and at the Council for Exceptional Children conference in April 2005, resulted in a draft template. Several iterations of the SOP were subsequently sent out to these representatives for review as well as to hundreds of state and local professionals. In the summer of 2005 a final version of the SOP, which incorporated the comments of a wide variety of stakeholders, was sent to the participating national organization representatives who formally participated in the development process. The participating organizations support the concept of providing a model that can be considered by states as they seek to develop their own procedures for complying with the IDEA requirements.

The IDEA 2004 did not prescribe any particular format or content for the Summary of Performance, allowing for local flexibility. The SOP model template can be found in Appendix 3 and is provided as an example to be adapted by state and local educational agencies.

How Can the SOP Help the Student?

First, the SOP is intended as a tool that the student can carry—like a passport—from secondary to postschool life. It presents an opportunity to merge a lot of information into a clear, understandable, and usable document that facilitates student self-determination. It can assist the student to break through the confusing language of assessment data and to obtain an understanding of current strengths, skills, and need for accommodations and supports. In order to maximize the potential use of the document, the narrative should be clear and understandable and written in positive, person-centered language. The second audience for the SOP is service providers in a range of postschool environments. The content of the document can provide these professionals with current, comprehensive, and meaningful information about the student's strengths, strategies used, and needs (Madaus, Bigaj, Chafouleas, & Simonsen, in press).

The SOP presents an unprecedented opportunity to send the student into postsecondary environments with a document that may bridge the gap between the results of standardized assessments and actual performance as measured by a variety of informal assessment data in a variety of contexts. It is important to note that the SOP is *not* a new set of evaluations and assessment data. Rather, as the name implies, it is a summary of existing data and of performance in academic and functional areas. These areas may include, but not be limited to, academic skills (e.g., reading, written language, math, learning skills); cognitive abilities (e.g., problem solving, attention, communication); and functional areas (e.g., social skills, independent living skills, self-determination skills, career/vocational skills).

The SOP offers secondary school personnel the chance to summarize the student's current strengths and weaknesses in each area. It also provides for a description of accommodations, modifications, and assistive technology applications that assist the student in the secondary environment. The description of accommodations and modifications should focus on those that have been recently used and have actually been effective for the student, rather than accommodations and modifications that were proposed but not effectively implemented. This information can be invaluable to enhance students' self-knowledge and self-advocacy as they move into new environments with new requirements and demands. Likewise, this information may provide service providers in two- and four-year postsecondary institutions with more comprehensive information regarding the student's level of performance than what was often available in traditional documentation (Madaus et al., 2006).

What Information Is Included in the SOP?

Because the SOP must apply to students with a range of disabilities transitioning to an array of diverse postsecondary environments, the relevant categories and the corresponding data will vary from student to student. In some cases, the suggested assessments and data will be primarily norm-referenced (standardized) and supplemented with informal assessments. For example, for some students transitioning to postsecondary education, the summary of academic and cognitive skills may be the most important section of the document. However, for some who will be working and living independently for the first time, consideration of the social skills and independent living skills may provide more valuable information for future planning. Previously, this information was rarely available in traditional psychoeducational reports. The SOP provides the vehicle to describe the student's strengths and weaknesses in this critical area. In comparison, many traditional norm-referenced assessments do not incorporate information or shed light on this critical life skill (Madaus et al., 2006). The Summary of Performance Template has five parts that are detailed below:

1. *Background and demographic information.* The information in this section provides a wide range of fundamental, but vital, data to personnel in postsecondary environments in a quick and efficient manner. It provides an important and useful summary of data that exiting students should be aware of, but frequently might not be. The section also provides a list of a wide range of formal and informal assessment methods that may have been compiled on a student. These assessments provide the data that clearly identifies the student's disability and functional strengths and needs. An initial scan of this list of areas can be overwhelming, as nineteen possible areas are provided. However, depending upon the student's disability and postsecondary goals, only some of these sections might be relevant. The section requests that only the most recent formal and informal assessment reports be attached (Madaus et al., 2006). Providing the actual reports is necessary if students are to fulfill the disability documentation requirements of many colleges.

2. *Student's postsecondary goals.* These goals should indicate the post-school environment(s) the student intends to transition to upon completion of high school, which could include employment, higher education, training, community participation, and/or independent living. This sets the direction for the focus of the contents of the remaining sections of the SOP. This section of the SOP template relates to the postschool environment(s) the student plans to transition to upon exiting high school. This information is already available in the transition IEP, which must include "appropriate measurable postsecondary goals based upon age appropriate transition assessments related to training, education, employment, and, where appropriate, independent living skills" (§300.320(b)). Thus, the information most essential to this section can be taken directly from these postsecondary goals. Because these goals drive the assessment data that is collected, it will be useful to reference them frequently as the SOP is developed (Madaus et al., 2006).

3. *Present level of performance.* By the time a student is preparing to exit secondary education, there will be a range of available assessment and school performance data. The Present Level of Performance section offers a chance to integrate the data to provide a current picture of the student's strengths and needs. How the information is distilled and analyzed into a profile of student strengths and challenges in light of postsecondary goals offers the true potential of the SOP. Other types of data that could be included in these statements include strategies and skills used by the student. For example, comments can be included related to the student's ability to work independently, or the type of instruction that the student seems to respond to most productively. This section also provides an opportunity to describe strategies and techniques used by the student to succeed in particular domains. Such data will likely be available in review of classroom observations and through discussions with teachers and students.

This section includes three critical areas: Academic, cognitive, and functional levels of performance. Academic areas include reading, math, language, and learning skills (e.g., note-taking, keyboarding, organization, time management, study skills, test-taking skills). It includes the student's present level of performance (grade level, standard scores, strengths, needs) and the accommodations, modifications, and assistive technology that were *essential* in high school to assist the student in achieving progress.

Essential Accommodations, Modifications, and Assistive Technology. The second column requests information regarding "Essential accommodations, modifications, and/or assistive technology utilized in high school and why needed." The inclusion of Essential Accommodations, Modifications, and Assistive Technology section provides secondary personnel with the opportunity to provide information about accommodations actually used and relevant for the student on a day-to-day basis. The student's Individualized Education Program (IEP) may list a series of recommendations related to accommodations and modifications that may not actually be used, or that were used previously, but did not prove to be effective.

The template defines an *accommodation* as a support or service that is provided to help a student fully access the general education curriculum or subject matter. An accommodation *does not change the content* of what is being taught or the expectation that the student meet a performance standard applied for all students. A *modification,* on the other hand, is defined as a change to the general education curriculum or other material being taught that alters the standards or expectations for students with disabilities. Instruction can be modified so that the material is presented differently and/or the expectations of what the student will master are changed. Most postsecondary education environments do not allow modifications because they indicate the student is not otherwise qualified. *Assistive technology* is defined as any device that helps a student with a disability function in a given environment, but does not limit the device to expensive or "high-tech" options.

Standardized test data may serve as the initial basis for a decision about why a particular accommodation or modification was needed. But there are also decisions made about accommodations or modifications on the basis of observational and other informal assessment data. It might be useful to gather the perspectives from the student and of a range from teachers to ascertain which accommodations and modifications were truly effective and why they were needed. The rationale for such decisions would be lost if only standardized assessment data was included in the SOP. This column provides a powerful means to provide practical information to both the student and postsecondary service providers with a rationale about why the accommodation or modification is essential (Madaus et al., 2006).

4. *Recommendations to assist the student in meeting postsecondary goals.* This section requires the secondary personnel to review the information in the Summary of Performance to predict what accommodations and supports will be useful in postsecondary settings. It is crucial that secondary personnel consider the differences between high school and postsecondary (e.g., employment, postsecondary education) settings as well as the differences in the requirements among IDEA, Section 504 of the Rehabilitation Act, and the Americans with Disabilities Act. Recommendations provided should not imply that any recommendations based on the high school experience will automatically qualify for services in the postsecondary education or the employment setting. Postsecondary settings will continue to make decisions regarding eligibility and needed accommodations on a case-by-case basis. Given that this could possibly create conflict between consumers and postsecondary personnel if recommendations are unrealistic, it is best to review the data to be sure that the recommendations are data-based and the accommodations or supports are available in post-high school settings. The recommendation that an individual be given unlimited time to complete assignments would likely not be available in most work settings. Similarly, recommendations for resource rooms,

special classes, or curriculum modifications are not allowed in most four-year colleges.

5. *Student input.* The student should actively participate in developing the SOP in collaboration with school professionals. The student's contribution can help (a) secondary professionals complete the summary, (b) the student to better understand the impact of his or her disability on academic and functional performance in the postsecondary setting, and (c) postsecondary personnel to more clearly understand the student's strengths and the impact of the disability. This part may be filled out independently by the student or completed with the student through an interview. It is important to remember that this document belongs to the student and its usefulness depends on the extent to which he or she understands and agrees with its contents.

Linking the SOP with the IEP Process

The Summary of Performance is a historical document, not the beginning of a student's postschool transition planning. Rather, this document is the culmination of a thoughtful and comprehensive transition plan that was initiated in the later stages of a student's middle school career or, at the latest, the early stages of high school. The student's postsecondary goals should be defined and based in age-appropriate transition assessments, as mandated in the regulations of the IDEA 2004. The student's secondary curriculum and transition plan should then be targeted toward reaching these goals. Data collection should be ongoing to measure progress in meeting these goals, and it is this data that will provide the foundation upon which the SOP should be developed.

The SOP is most useful when linked with the IEP process, and the student has the opportunity to actively participate in the development of this document. The transition coordinator, special educator, or guidance counselor who develops the SOP should typically be someone who knows the student. The IEP team, possibly through the transition planning process, should identify this professional in a timely manner so the SOP can be "built" over time (i.e., relevant formal and informal assessments can be identified and placed in the student's file; accommodations on high-stakes tests specified in the IEP can be determined so their use and effectiveness can be determined and reported). The IEP coordinator should consult the student, parents, and other professionals (e.g., teachers, related services personnel) to complete all the relevant parts of the document. A final draft of the SOP should be presented to the IEP team for its review, revision, and formal approval.

What Is the Timeline for Producing an SOP?

The SOP must be completed during the final year of a student's high school education. Although it would be easier for the IEP team to set a specific time for completing the SOP, it would be best to vary the timing for completion of the SOP based upon the individual needs of the student as specified in the Transition Plan. This will vary, depending on the student's postsecondary goals. If a student is transitioning to higher education, the SOP, with additional documentation, may be necessary as the student applies to a college or university. Likewise, this information may be necessary as a student applies for services from state agencies such as vocational rehabilitation. In some instances, it may be most appropriate to wait until the spring of a student's final year to provide an agency or employer the most updated information on the performance of the student prior to graduation.

The Summary of Performance Model Template

A model SOP template (Appendix 3), developed by the National Transition Documentation Summit, reflects the contributions and suggestions of numerous stakeholders in professional organizations, school districts, universities, and state departments of education. *A specific form has not been mandated by IDEA or the Department of Education,* so this template is intended to be shared, adapted, and modified to fit the unique needs of state and local educational systems. It is available to be freely copied or adapted for educational purposes (Shaw, Kochhar-Bryant, Izzo, Benedict, & Parker, 2005).

Closing

In the first decade of this new millennium, the journey toward achieving improved transition outcomes for our nation's youths is only just beginning. This is an era of great experimentation in education and employment preparation that will profoundly affect the lives of youths with disabilities well into this new century. There is a heightened national effort to identify promising and best practices in education that promote successful transition. The concept of transition as a comprehensive unified planning framework for youths undergirds these promising practices. National investment in transition demonstrates to the nation and the world a national commitment to the welfare, self-determination, and full participation of all youths in their communities.

APPENDIX 1: *IDEA 1997 and 2004: Comparison of Provisions Related to Transition*

IDEA 1997	IDEA 2004

PART A: GENERAL PROVISIONS

SECTION 601: Short Title; Table of Contents; Findings; Purposes	**Section 601: Short Title; Table of Contents; Findings; Purposes**
(d) PURPOSES. The purposes of this title are—	(d) PURPOSES. The purposes of this title are—
(1)(A) to ensure that all children with disabilities have available to them a free appropriate public education that emphasizes special education and related services designed to meet their unique needs and prepare them for employment and independent living	(1)(A) to ensure that all children with disabilities have available to them a free appropriate public education that emphasizes special education and related services designed to meet their unique needs and prepare them **for further education,** employment, and independent living
SECTION 602: Definitions	**SECTION 602: Definitions**
(30) TRANSITION SERVICES. The term "transition services" means a coordinated set of activities for a student with disability that—	(34) TRANSITION SERVICES: The term "transition services" means a coordinated set of activities for a **child** with a disability that—
(A) is designed within an outcome-oriented process, which promotes movement from school to post-school activities, including post-secondary education, vocational training, integrated employment (including supported employment), continuing and adult education, adult services, independent living, or community participation;	(A) is designed to be **within a results**-oriented process, **that is focused on improving the academic and functional achievement of the child with a disability to facilitate the child's** movement from school to post-school activities, including post-secondary education, vocational **education,** integrated employment (including supported employment), continuing and adult education, adult services, independent living, or community participation;
(B) is based upon the individual student's needs, taking into account the student's preferences and interests; and	(B) is based on the individual child's needs, taking into account the **child's strengths,** preferences, and interests; and
(C) includes instruction, related services, community experiences, the development of employment and other post-school adult living objectives, and when appropriate, acquisition of daily living skills and functional vocational evaluation.	(C) includes instruction, related services, community experiences, the development of employment and other post-school adult living objectives, and when appropriate, acquisition of daily living skills and functional vocational evaluation.

PART B: ASSISTANCE FOR EDUCATION OF ALL CHILDREN WITH DISABILITIES

IDEA 1997	IDEA 2004
SECTION 614: Individualized Education Programs	**SECTION 614: Individualized Education Programs**
(c) ADDITIONAL REQUIREMENTS FOR EVALUATION AND REEVALUATIONS	(c) ADDITIONAL REQUIREMENTS FOR EVALUATION AND REEVALUATIONS
(5) EVALUATIONS BEFORE CHANGE IN ELIGIBILITY—A local educational agency shall evaluate a child with a disability in accordance with this section before determining that the child is no longer a child with a disability.	(5) EVALUATIONS BEFORE CHANGE IN ELIGIBILITY—
	(A) IN GENERAL—**Except as provided in subparagraph (B)**, a local educational agency shall evaluate a child with a disability in accordance with this section before determining that the child is no longer a child with a disability.
	(B) EXCEPTION—
	(i) IN GENERAL—The evaluation described in subparagraph (A) shall not be required before the termination of a child's eligibility under this part due to graduation from secondary school with a regular diploma, or due to exceeding the age eligibility for a free appropriate public education under State law.
	(ii) SUMMARY OF PERFORMANCE—For a child whose eligibility under this part terminates under circumstances described in clause (i), a local education agency shall provide the child with a summary of the child's academic achievement and functional performance, which shall include recommendations on how to assist the child in meeting the child's postsecondary goals.

86

IDEA 1997	IDEA 2004
SECTION 614: Individualized Education Programs	**SECTION 614: Individualized Education Programs**
(d) INDIVIDUALIZED EDUCATION PROGRAMS	(d) INDIVIDUALIZED EDUCATION PROGRAMS
(1) DEFINITIONS	(1) DEFINITIONS
(A) INDIVIDUALIZED EDUCATION PROGRAM	(A) INDIVIDUALIZED EDUCATION PROGRAM
(vii)(I) beginning at age 14, and updated annually, a statement of the transition service needs of the child under the applicable components of the child's IEP that focuses on the child's courses of study (such as participation in advanced-placement courses or a vocational education program);	**(VII) the projected date for the beginning of services and modifications, the anticipated frequency, location and duration of those services. . . .**
(II) beginning at age 16 (or younger, if determined appropriate by the IEP Team), a statement of needed transition services for the child, including, when appropriate, a statement of the interagency responsibilities or any needed linkages; and	**(VIII) beginning not later that the first IEP to be in effect when the child is 16, and updated annually thereafter—** *
(III) beginning at least one year before the child reaches the age of majority under State law, a statement that the child has been informed of his or her rights under this title, if any, that will transfer to the child on reaching the age of majority under section 615(m); and	**(aa) appropriate measurable postsecondary goals based upon age appropriate transition assessments related to training, education, employment, and, where appropriate, independent living skills;**
(viii) a statement of—	**(bb) the transition services (including courses of study) needed to assist the child in reaching those goals; and**
(I) how the child's progress toward the annual goals described in clause	(cc) beginning **not later than** 1 year before the child reaches the age of majority under State law, a statement that the child has been informed of the child's rights under this title, if any, that will transfer to the child on reaching the age of majority under section 615(m).
(ii) will be measured; and	**(ii) RULE OF CONSTRUCTION— nothing in this section shall be construed to require—**
	(I) that additional information be included in a child's IEP beyond what is explicitly required in this section; and

*The following text appears in the Proposed Rules, 300.320(b), June 2005: ''Beginning with the first IEP in effect after the child turns age 16, or younger than age 16 if determined appropriate by the IEP team.

87

PART B: Continued

IDEA 1997	IDEA 2004
(II) how the child's parents will be regularly informed (by such means as periodic report cards), at least as often as parents are informed of their nondisabled children's progress of—	(II) the IEP Team to include information under 1 component of a child's IEP that is already contained under another component of such IEP.
(aa) their child's progress toward the annual goals described in clause (ii); and	[Note: The following text appears in Part B, Section 614 (d)(1)(A)(i), as part of the definition of what an IEP includes.]
(bb) the extent to which that progress is sufficient to enable the child to achieve the goals by the end of the year.	(II) a statement of measurable annual goals, including academic and functional goals, designed to—
	(aa) meet the child's needs that result from the child's disability to enable the child to be involved in and make progress in the general education curriculum; and
	(bb) meet each of the child's other educational needs that result from the child's disability;
	(III) a description of how the child's progress toward meeting the annual goals described in subclause (II) will be measured and when periodic reports on the progress the child is making toward meeting the annual goals (such as through the use of quarterly or other periodic reports, concurrent with the issuance of report card) will be provided.
	(D)(6). If a participating agency, fails to provide the transition services described in the IEP, the local educational agency shall reconvene the IEP team to identify strategies to meet the transition objectives for the child set out in the IEP.

IDEA 1997	IDEA 2004
(3) DEVELOPMENT OF IEP—	(3) DEVELOPMENT OF IEP—
(A) IN GENERAL—In developing each child's IEP, the IEP Team, subject to subparagraph (C), shall consider –	(A) IN GENERAL—In developing each child's IEP, the IEP Team, subject to subparagraph (C), shall consider—
(i) the strengths of the child and the concerns of the parents for enhancing the education of their child; and	(i) the strengths of the child;
(ii) the results of the initial evaluation or most recent evaluation of the child.	(ii) the concerns of the parents for enhancing the education of their child;
	(iii) the results of the initial evaluation or most recent evaluation of the child; and
	(iv) the academic, developmental, and functional needs of the child.
	The IEP team **shall consider special factors** for children:
	• whose **behavior** impedes learning
	• who have **limited English proficiency**
	• who are **blind or visually impaired**
	• who are **deaf or hard of hearing** (Section 1414(d)(3)(B))
Multi-Year IEPs:	Multi-Year IEPs:
(No comparative language)	Fifteen states may request approval to implement optional "comprehensive, multi-year IEPs" for periods of no longer than three years. IEP review dates must be based on "natural transition points."
	Parents have the right to opt-out of this program. The parent of a child served under a multi-year IEP can request a review of the IEP without waiting for the "natural transition point." (Section 1414(d)(5))

89

PART B: Continued

IDEA 1997	IDEA 2004
(6) CHILDREN WITH DISABILITIES IN ADULT PRISONS—	(7) CHILDREN WITH DISABILITIES IN ADULT PRISONS—
(A) IN GENERAL—The following requirements do not apply to children with disabilities who are convicted as adults under State law and incarcerated in adult prisons:	(A) IN GENERAL—The following requirements shall not apply to children with disabilities who are convicted as adults under State law and incarcerated in adult prisons:
(i) The requirements contained in section 612(a)(17) and paragraph (1)(A)(v) of this subsection (relating to participation of children with disabilities in general assessments.)	(i) The requirements contained in section 612(a)(16) and paragraph(1)(A)(i)(VI) (relating to participation of children with disabilities in general assessments).
(ii) The requirements of subclauses (I) and (II) of paragraph (1)(A)(vii) of this subsection (relating to transition planning and transition services), do not apply with respect to such children whose eligibility under this part will end, because of their age, before they will be released from prison.	(ii) The requirements of items (aa) and (bb) of paragraph (1)(A)(i)(VIII) (relating to transition planning and transition services), do not apply with respect to such children whose eligibility under this part will end, because of **such children's age, before such children** will be released from prison.

90

APPENDIX 2: *The No Child Left Behind Act of 2001: Provisions Related to Transition*

Provisions	Comment
TITLE I. IMPROVING THE ACADEMIC ACHIEVEMENT OF THE DISADVANTAGED **Part C. Education of Migratory Children** **Sec. 1301 Program Purpose** (5) design programs to help migratory children overcome educational disruption, cultural and language barriers, social isolation, health-related problems and other factors that inhibit the ability of such children to do well in school, and to prepare such children to make a successful transition to postsecondary education or employment.	At-risk youths are more likely than their peers to drop out of school, experience educational failure, or be involved in activities that are detrimental to their health and safety. Available research shows that children raised in economically disadvantaged families are at greater risk of low academic achievement, behavioral problems, poor health, and have difficulties with adjustments to adulthood (Hale, 1998; Land & Legters, 2002).
Part D. Prevention and Intervention Programs for Children and Youth Who Are Neglected, Delinquent, or At-Risk **Sec. 1402 Purpose and Program Authorization** (2) to provide such children and youth with the services needed to make a successful transition from institutionalization to further schooling or employment; (3) to prevent at-risk youth from dropping out of school, and to provide dropouts, and children and youth returning from correctional facilities or institutions for neglected or delinquent children and youth, with a support system to ensure their continued education	Provides transitions out of institutions into home schools. Nearly one-third of the U.S. adult population does not advance beyond high school and this proportion has remained relatively constant for nearly 30 years according to Friedman (2000). It is estimated that approximately one million youth per year leave school without completing their basic educational requirements (Barr & Parrett, 2001). Adolescents with emotional and behavioral disabilities (EBD) have only a 41.9 percent graduation rate and the highest dropout rate of any disability category (U.S. Department of Education, 2001).
Section 1414 State Plan and State Agency Applications (B) for assisting in the transition of children and youth from correctional facilities to locally operated programs;	Strengthens transition services and supports for youths transferring into the community from correctional facilities such as adult jails, juvenile detention, less secure detention facilities, or protective shelters.

The No Child Left Behind Act of 2001: Provisions Related to Transition (continued)

Provisions	Comment
Section 1415 Use of Funds	Strengthens the ability of youths exiting correctional facilities to enter postsecondary education or employment.
(B) concentrate on providing participants with the knowledge and skills needed to make a successful transition to secondary school completion, vocational or technical training, further education or employment.	
Section 1416 Institution-Wide Projects	The school district program is required to attend to the transition and academic needs of students returning from correctional facilities. Often, there is a disconnect between the local schools and correctional facilities, which results in low student achievement or dropout. As students transition back to their local schools, follow-up services can ensure that their education continues and they can meet the same challenging state standards required of all students.
(3) describes the steps the State agency has taken, or will take, to provide all children and youth under age 21 with the opportunity to meet challenging State academic content standards and student academic achievement standards in order to improve the likelihood that the children and youth will complete secondary school, attain a secondary diploma or its recognized equivalent, or find employment after leaving the institution.	
Section 1418 Transition Services	Youths with disabilities are substantially overrepresented in the juvenile justice system (Rutherford & Quinn, 1999). Youths with specific learning, emotional or behavioral disabilities are more vulnerable to alternative placement outside their base school or in juvenile or adult corrections than youths not identified as disabled. Youths placed at risk for involvement in the juvenile justice system, including students with disabilities, must receive support and preventive services to minimize their vulnerability.
Transition services—Each State agency shall reserve not less than 15 percent and not more than 30 percent of the amount the agency receives for any fiscal year to support—	
(1) projects that facilitate the transition of children and youth from State-operated institutions to schools served by local educational agencies; or	Ethnic minorities are dramatically overrepresented in the population of young offenders. A study conducted from 1988–1997 of youths held in public and private juvenile detention, correctional, and shelter facilities
(2) the successful reentry of youth offenders, who are age 20 or younger and have received a secondary school diploma or its recognized equivalent, into postsecondary education, or vocational and technical training program, through strategies designed to expose the youth to, and prepare the youth for postsecondary education, or vocational and technical training programs, such as—	

92

The No Child Left Behind Act of 2001: Provisions Related to Transition (continued)

Provisions	Comment
(A) preplacement programs that allow adjudicated or incarcerated youth to audit or attend courses on college, university or community college campuses, or through programs provided in the institution;	revealed that more than three-quarters (86.5%) of the 105,000 juveniles studies were young men from ethnic minority backgrounds (40% Black and 18.5% Hispanic) ranging in age from 13 to 17 years old.
(A) worksite schools, in which institutions of higher education and private or public employers partner to created programs to help students make a successful transition to postsecondary education and employment;	
(A) essential support services to ensure the success of youth, such as—personal, vocational, technical and academic counseling; placement services designed to place the youth in a university, college or junior college program; counseling services, and job placement services.	
TITLE V. PROMOTING INFORMED PARENTAL CHOICE AND INNOVATIVE PROGRAMS	Women and children account for more than three-quarters of households with incomes below the poverty level. Children from racial minority groups are much more likely to live in poverty than are white children. Unmarried teen mothers need access to day care, transportation, and other supports that will enable them to work and pursue their education (National Council for Research on Women, 2001, 1998).
Subpart 21 Women's Educational Equity Act	
Sec. 5611 (2) Support and Technical Assistance	
(A) (iv) school to work transition programs, guidance and counseling activities, and other programs to increase opportunities for women and girls to enter a technologically demanding workplace and, in particular to enter highly skills, high paying careers in which women and girls have been under-represented;	

93

The No Child Left Behind Act of 2001: Provisions Related to Transition (continued)

Provisions	Comment
TITLE VII. INDIAN, NATIVE HAWAIIAN, AND ALASKA NATIVE EDUCATION Subpart 2—Special Programs and Project to Improve Educational Opportunities for Indian Children Sec. 7121 Improvement of Educational Opportunities for Indian Children (C) Grants Authorized (E) special compensatory and other programs and projects designed to assist and encourage Indian children to enter, remain in, or reenter school, and to increase the rate of high school graduation; (F) comprehensive guidance, counseling and testing services; (H) partnership programs between local educational agencies and institutions of higher education that allow secondary school students to enroll in courses at the post-secondary level to aid such students in the transition from secondary to post-secondary education; (I) partnership projects between schools and local businesses for career preparation programs designed to provide Indian youth with the knowledge and skills such youth need to make an effective transition from school to a high-skill wage career.	Native American students with disabilities face unique challenges to successful transition. Chemical dependency, lack of familial support, and lack of support networks for students with disabilities who enter higher education institutions, all play a role in the high dropout rates and the challenges in transitioning into adulthood successfully. In addition, other factors such as lack of employment opportunities, limited resources, and high poverty levels impede the ability of Native Americans to succeed in higher education and independent living. Employment rates run as high as 70% in some reservations, putting Native American youth, as a whole, at a heightened risk for failure to assume adult roles and responsibilities after leaving high school (Blasi, 2001; Leake, Kim-Rupnow & Leung, 2003; Shafer & Rangasamy, 1995).

94

APPENDIX 3A: *Summary of Performance Model Template*

This template was developed by the National Transition Documentation Summit © 2005 based on the initial work of Stan Shaw, Carol Kochhar-Bryant, Margo Izzo, Ken Benedict, and David Parker. It reflects the contributions and suggestions of numerous stakeholders in professional organizations, school districts, and universities. It is available to be freely copied or adapted for educational purposes. Participating organizations include the Council for Exceptional Children's Division on Career Development and Transition (DCDT), Division on Learning Disabilities (DLD), and Council on Educational Diagnostic Services (CEDS), Learning Disability Association (LDA), the Higher Education Consortium for Special Education (HECSE), and the Council for Learning Disabilities (CLD). *[It can also be accessed on the CEC website, http://www.cec.sped.org/pp/pdfs/SOP.pdf]*

Part 1: Background Information

Student Name: _____

Date of Birth: _____ Year of Graduation/Exit: _____

Address: _____

   (Street)   (Town, state)   (Zip code)

Telephone Number: _____ Primary Language: _____

Current School: _____ City: _____

Student's primary disability (Diagnosis): _____

Student's secondary disability (Diagnosis), if applicable: _____

When was the student's disability (or disabilities) formally diagnosed? _____

If English is not the student's primary language, what services were provided for this student as an English language learner?

_____

Date of most recent IEP or most recent 504 plan: _____

Date this Summary was completed: _____

This form was completed by: Name: _____

Title: _____

School: _____ E-mail: _____

Telephone Number: _____

Please check and include the most recent copy of assessment reports that you are attaching that diagnose and clearly identify the student's disability or functional limitations and/or information that will assist in postsecondary planning:

- ❏ Psychological/cognitive
- ❏ Response to Intervention (RTI)
- ❏ Neuropsychological
- ❏ Language proficiency assessments
- ❏ Medical/physical
- ❏ Reading assessments
- ❏ Achievement/academics
- ❏ Communication
- ❏ Adaptive behavior
- ❏ Behavioral analysis
- ❏ Social/interpersonal skills
- ❏ Classroom observations (or in other settings)
- ❏ Community-based assessment
- ❏ Career/vocational or transition assessment
- ❏ Self-determination
- ❏ Assistive technology
- ❏ Informal assessment: _____
- ❏ Informal assessment: _____
- ❏ Other: _____

Part 2: Student's Postsecondary Goal(s)

1. _____
_____
_____
_____

2. _____
_____
_____
_____

3. _____
_____
_____
_____

If employment is the primary goal, the top three job interests: _____
_____
_____
_____

Part 3: Summary of Performance
(Complete all that are relevant to the student)

ACADEMIC CONTENT AREAS	Present Level of Performance (Grade level, standard scores, strengths, needs)	*Essential* accommodations, modifications, and/or assistive technology utilized in high school and why needed
Reading (Basic reading/decoding; reading comprehension; reading speed)		
Math (Calculation skills, algebraic problem solving; quantitative reasoning)		
Language (written expression, speaking, spelling)		
Learning Skills (class participation, note taking, keyboarding, organization, homework management, time management, study skills, test-taking skills)		

COGNITIVE AREAS	Present Level of Performance (Grade level, standard scores, strengths, needs)	*Essential* accommodations, modifications, and/or assistive technology utilized in high school and why needed
General Ability and Problem Solving (reasoning/processing)		
Attention and Executive Functioning (energy level, sustained attention, memory functions, processing speed, impulse control activity level)		
Communication (speech/language, assisted communication)		

FUNCTIONAL AREAS	Present Level of Performance (Grade level, standard scores, strengths and needs)	*Essential* accommodations, modifications, and/or assistive technology utilized in high school and why needed
Social Skills and Behavior (interactions with teachers/peers, level of initiation in asking for assistance, responsiveness to services and accommodations, degree of involvement in extra-curricular activities, confidence and persistence as a learner)		
Independent Living Skills (self-care, leisure skills, personal safety, transportation, banking, budgeting)		
Environmental Access/Mobility (assistive technology, mobility, transportation)		
Self-Determination/ Self-Advocacy Skills (ability to identify and articulate postsecondary goals, learning strengths and needs)		
Career-Vocational/ Transition/Employment (career interests, career exploration, job training, employment experiences and supports)		
Additional important considerations that can assist in making decisions about disability determination and needed accommodations (e.g., medical problems, family concerns, sleep disturbance)		

Part 4: Recommendations to Assist the Student in Meeting Postsecondary Goals

Suggestions for accommodations, adaptive devices, assistive services, compensatory strategies, and/or collateral support services, to enhance access in the following post-high school environments (only complete those relevant to the student's postsecondary goals).

Higher Education or Career-Technical Education: _____

Employment: _____

Independent Living: _____

Community Participation: _____

Part 5: Student Input (Highly Recommended)

Summary of Performance: Student Perspective

A. How does your disability affect your schoolwork and school activities (such as grades, relationships, assignments, projects, communication, time on tests, mobility, extra-curricular activities)?

B. In the past, what supports have been tried by teachers or by you to help you succeed in school (aids, adaptive equipment, physical accommodations, other services)?

C. Which of these accommodations and supports has worked best for you?

D. Which of these accommodations and supports have not worked?

E. What strengths and needs should professionals know about you as you enter the postsecondary education or work environment?

I have reviewed and agree with the content of this Summary of Performance.

Student Signature: _____ Date: _____

APPENDIX 3B: *Example Summary of Performance*

Student with a Learning Disability

This template was developed by the National Transition Documentation Summit © 2005 based on the initial work of Stan Shaw, Carol Kochhar-Bryant, Margo Izzo, Ken Benedict, and David Parker. It reflects the contributions and suggestions of numerous stakeholders in professional organizations, school districts, and universities, particularly the Connecticut Interagency Transition Task Force. It is available to be freely copied or adapted for educational purposes. The model template has been formally ratified by the Council for Exceptional Children's Division on Career Development and Transition (DCDT), Division on Learning Disabilities (DLD), and Council on Educational Diagnostic Services (CEDS), Learning Disability Association (LDA), the Higher Education Consortium for Special Education (HECSE), and the Council for Learning Disabilities (CLD).

Part 1: Background Information

Student Name: _____Chris Miles_____

Date of Birth: _____8-17-88_____ Year of Graduation/Exit: ___2006___

Address: _____

      (Street)   (Town, state)   (Zip code)

Telephone Number:_____ Primary Language: _____

Current School: _____ City: _____

Student's primary disability (Diagnosis): _____

Student's secondary disability (Diagnosis), if applicable: _____

When was the student's disability (or disabilities) formally diagnosed? ____9_____

If English is not the student's primary language, what services were provided for this student as an English language learner?_____

Date of most recent IEP or most recent 504 plan: _____2005_____

Date this Summary was completed: _____Jan. 2007_____

This form was completed by: Name: _____Ed Reviewer_____

Title: _____School Psychologist_____

School: ___Fairlawn High School___ E-mail: _Review_Ed@fairlawn.org_

Telephone Number: _____614-223-XXXX_____

100

Please check and include the most recent copy of assessment reports that you are attaching that diagnose and clearly identify the student's disability or functional limitations and/or that will assist in postsecondary planning:

- ■ Psychological/cognitive
- ❏ Response to Intervention (RTI)
- ❏ Neuropsychological
- ❏ Language proficiency assessments
- ❏ Medical/physical
- ■ Reading assessments
- ■ Achievement/academics
- ❏ Communication
- ❏ Adaptive behavior
- ❏ Behavioral analysis
- ■ Social/interpersonal skills
- ❏ Classroom observations (or in other settings)
- ❏ Community-based assessment
- ❏ Career/vocational or transition assessment
- ❏ Self-determination
- ❏ Assistive technology
- ❏ Informal assessment: _____
- ❏ Informal assessment: _____
- ■ Other: _____ Multi-factored team report _____

Part 2: Student's Postsecondary Goal(s)

1. Attend a four-year college

2. Utilize Disability services at college to gain access to assistive technology, extended time on tests and a notetaker

3. Part-time employment during school and full-time employment after college

If employment is the primary goal, the top three job interests: _____
_____ Business, Sales, Retail Distribution _____
_____
_____

101

Part 3: Summary of Performance
(Complete all that are relevant to the student)

ACADEMIC CONTENT AREAS	Present Level of Performance (Grade level, standard scores, strengths, needs)	*Essential* accommodations, modifications and/or assistive technology utilized in high school and why needed
Reading (Basic reading/decoding; reading comprehension; reading speed)	Reading comprehension—5th grade. Reading level improves if assistive technology is used to assist with decoding and content is presented through auditory means.	Books on Tape or MP3 player. AT such as Wynn or Read and Write Gold. 50% extended time on exams requiring reading.
Math (calculation skills, algebraic problem solving; quantitative reasoning)	6th grade math level for calculations and problem solving.	Talking calculator to assist with transfer issues.
Language (written expression, speaking, spelling)	Spells phonetically and reverses the sounds when writing. Needs assistance with grammar.	Assistive technology such as Wynn or Read and Write Gold to check what is written.
Learning Skills (class participation, note taking, keyboarding, organization, homework management, time management, study skills, test-taking skills)	Excellent class participation and verbal communication skills. Chris always does homework but accuracy is an issue: Problems with written expression and attention to detail result in frequent mistakes in spelling and math.	A notetaker is needed to compensate for the visual processing disorder that that affects written expression.

COGNITIVE AREAS	Present Level of Performance (grade level, standard scores, strengths, needs)	*Essential* accommodations, modifications and/or assistive technology utilized in high school and why needed
General Ability and Problem Solving (reasoning/processing)	Sequential order difficulty but overall good reasoning ability.	*Needs assistance with prioritizing assignments.*
Attention and Executive Functioning (energy level, sustained attention, memory functions, processing speed, impulse control, activity level)	Good auditory memory and stays on task when working on a project or assignment.	
Communication (speech/language, assisted communication)	Excellent auditory and speaking skills.	

FUNCTIONAL AREAS	Present Level of Performance (Strengths and needs)	*Essential* accommodations/ modifications and/or assistive technology utilized in high school and why needed
Social Skills and Behavior (interactions with teachers/peers, level of initiation in asking for assistance, responsiveness to services and accommodations, degree of involvement in extracurricular activities, confidence and persistence as a learner,)	Chris has strong social skills but may need assistance in asking for assistance when needed. Chris has participated in the drama club.	
Independent Living Skills (self-care, leisure skills, personal safety, transportation, banking, budgeting)	May need assistance with banking and budgeting—accuracy is an issue.	Chris has been encouraged to use a calculator and his natural support network.
Environmental Access/Mobility (assistive technology, mobility, transportation)	Uses assistive technology for reading and writing.	Assistive technology is an essential accommodation for reading and writing.
Self-Determination/ Self-Advocacy Skills (ability to identify and articulate postsecondary goals, learning strengths and needs;	Capable of identifying disability but does not ask for assistance when needed. Has difficulty explaining the functional limitations of his disability.	Quarterly meetings with a disability intervention specialist to determine appropriate accommodations for each college class.
Career-Vocational/ Transition/Employment (career interests, career exploration, job training, employment experiences and supports)	Chris has worked in retail positions and sales clerk. Assistance needed with resume writing and job application process.	
Additional important considerations that can assist in making decisions about disability determination and needed accommodations (e.g., medical problems, family concerns, sleep disturbance)		

Part 4: Recommendations to Assist the Student in Meeting Postsecondary Goals

Suggestions for accommodations, adaptive devices, assistive services, compensatory strategies, and/or collateral support services to enhance access in the following post-high school environments (only complete those relevant to the student's postsecondary goals).

Higher Education or Career-Technical Education:	Assistive technology to assist with reading and writing. Books on tape or MP3 player. Notetaker to compensate for the visual processing disorder and difficulty with the hand-eye coordination that affects written expression.
Employment:	Assistance with the employment application and developing cover letters.
Independent Living:	None.
Community Participation:	None.

Part 5: Student Input (Highly Recommended)

Summary of Performance: Student Perspective

A. How does your disability affect your schoolwork and school activities (such as grades, relationships, assignments, projects, communication, time on tests, mobility, extra-curricular activities)?

    I need to use my assistive technology and books on tape/
    MP3 players for reading and writing. I do better when
    information is presented in a concrete manner and I
    clarify what the requirements of an assignment are. I do
    better on verbal presentations than written papers.

B. In the past, what supports have been tried by teachers or by you to help you succeed in school (aids, adaptive equipment, physical accommodations, other services)?

    I have exchanged verbal presentations and projects for
    written papers. I meet with my teacher on a weekly basis
    to get help with prioritizing assignments. I meet with my
    tutor prior to tests and use my assistive technology on a
    daily basis. I also use a notetaker for lecture types of
    classes.

C. Which of these accommodations and supports has worked best for you?

    Assistive technology and a notetaker has worked best for
    me.

D. Which of these accommodations and supports have not worked?

    Dragon AT (speech-to-text) has not worked well.

E. What strengths and needs should professionals know about you as you enter the postsecondary education or work environment?

```
I have excellent communication skills and can present in
front of the class very well. I plan on using these
skills for my future employment in either a business
setting or in sales.
```

I have reviewed and agree with the content of this Summary of Performance.

Student Signature: _____**Chris Miles**_____ Date: _____1/6/06_____

References

Abery, B., & Stancliffe, R. (1996). The ecology of self-determination. In D. J. Sands & M. L. Wehmeyer (Eds.), *Self-determination across the life span: Independence and choice for people with disabilities* (pp. 111–146). Baltimore: Paul H. Brookes.

Americans with Disabilities Act of 1990, P.L. 101-336, 42 U.S.C. 12101 (1991).

Barr, R. D., & Parrett, W. H. (2001). *Hope fulfilled for at-risk and violent youth: K–12 programs that work.* Boston: Allyn and Bacon.

Bates, P., Suter, C., & Poelvoorde, R. (1986). *Illinois transition plan: Final report.* Chicago: Governor's Planning Council on Developmental Disabilities.

Benz, M., Lindstrom, L., & Yovonoff, P. (2000). Improving graduation and employment outcomes of students with disabilities: Predictive factors and student perspectives. *Exceptional Children, 6*(4), 509–529.

Berman, P., McLaughlin, M., Bass-Golod, G., Pauley, E., & Zellman, E. (1977). *Federal programs supporting educational change. Vol. VII, Factors affecting implementation and continuation.* Washington, DC: HEW. R-1589/7-HEW.

Berry, H., & Jones, M. (2000). *Social Security Disability Insurance and Supplemental Security Income for undergraduates with disabilities: An Analysis of the National Postsecondary Student Aid Survey* (NPSAS 2000), Washington, DC: GPO.

Blalock, G., & Benz, M. (1999). *Using community transition teams to improve transition services* (Pro-Ed Series on Transition). Austin, TX: Pro-Ed.

Blanck, P. D. (Ed.). (2000). *Employment, disability, and the Americans with Disabilities Act: Issues in law, public policy, and research.* Evanston, IL: Northwestern University Press.

Blasi, M. (2001). *Returning to the reservation: Experiences of a first year Native American teacher.* Washington, DC: Office of Educational Research and Improvement.

Bremer, C., Clapper, A., Hitchcock, C., Hall, T., & Kachgal, M. (December, 2002). Universal design: A strategy to support students' access to the general education curriculum information. *Brief Addressing Trends and Developments in Secondary Education and Transition, 1*(3). National Center for Secondary Education and Transition.

Bremer, C., Kachgal, M., & Schoeller, K. (April, 2003). Self-determination: Supporting successful transition. *Research to Practice Brief: Improving Secondary Education and Transition Services through Research, 2,* 91.

Brown, D. S. (2000). *Learning a living: A guide to planning your career and finding a job for people with learning disabilities, attention deficit disorder, and dyslexia.* Bethesda, MD: Woodbine House.

Bulgren, J. A., & Knackendoffel, A. (1986). Ecological assessment: An overview. *The Pointer, 30*(2), 23–30.

Cameto, R., Marder, C., Wagner, M., & Cardoso, D. (2003). Youth employment: NLTS2 Data Brief. *Report from the National Longitudinal Transition Study, 2*(2).

Career Education Implementation Incentive Act (P.L. 95-207).

Casper, B., & Leuchovius, D. (2005). *Universal design for learning and the transition to a more challenging academic curriculum: Making it in middle school and beyond.* Minneapolis, MN: National Center for Secondary Education and Transition.

Center for Applied Special Technology. (2004). *Universal design for learning.* Wakefield, MA: CAST. Accessed 12/29/05 from http://www.cast.org/about/index.cfm?i=231.

Center on Education Policy. (2003). *From the capitol to the classroom: State and federal efforts to implement the No Child Left Behind Act.* Washington, DC.

Center for Universal Design. (1997). *What is Universal Design?* Retrieved 12/27/05, from http://www.design.ncsu.edu/cud/univ_design/ud.htm.

Clark, G. M. (1998). *Assessment for transition planning.* Austin, TX: Pro-Ed.

Clark, G. M., Sitlington, P., & Kolstoe, O. P. (2000). *Transition education and services for adolescents with disabilities* (3rd ed.). Boston: Allyn and Bacon.

Covey, S. (2004). *The seven habits of highly effective people.* New York: The Free Press.

Cox, S., & Osguthorpe, R. T. (2003). How do instructional design professionals spend their time? *Tech Trends.*

Crane, K., Gramloch, M., & Peterson, K. (September, 2004). Putting interagency agreements into action, 3(2), Minneapolis: National Center for Secondary Education and Transition, University of Minnesota.

Defur, S. (2002). *Transition Summary 10* (TS10). Washington, DC: National Information Center for Children and Youth With Disabilities (NICHY).

DeFur, S. (2000). *Designing individualized education program (IEP) transition plans* (ERIC Digest E598). Arlington, VA: ERIC Clearinghouse on Disabilities and Gifted Education.

Destafano, L., Heck, D., Hazasi, S., & Furney, K. (1999). Enhancing the implementation of the transition requirements of IDEA: A report on the policy forum on transition. *Career Development for Exceptional Children, 22*(1), 85–100.

DeStefano, L., & Wermuth, T. (1992). IDEA (P.L. 101-476): Defining a second generation of transition services. In F. Rusch, L. DeStefano, J. Chadsey-Rusch, L. A. Phelps, & E. Szymanski (Eds.), *Transition from school to adult life* (pp. 537–549). Pacific Grove, CA: Brooks/Cole Publishing Company.

Dunst, C., & Bruder, M. (2002). Valued outcomes of service coordination, early intervention, and natural environments. *University of Connecticut Health Center, 68*(3), 361–375. Council for Exceptional Children.

Education for All Handicapped Children Act (P.L. 94-142, 20 U.S.C. 1401 et seq.), 1975.

Education of the Handicapped Act Amendments of 1983, P.L. 98-199. (1983).

Education Policy Reform Research Institute. (2004). *Ensuring accountability for all children in an era of standards-based reform: Alternate achievement standards.* Arlington, VA: Author.

Eisenman, L. T., & Chamberlin, M. (2001). Implementing self-determination activities: Lessons from schools. *Remedial and Special Education, 22,* 138–147.

Fabian, E. S., Lent, R. L., & Willis, S. P. (1998). Predicting work transition outcomes for students with disabilities: Implications for counselors. *Journal of Counseling & Development, 76,* 311–315.

Field, S., Hoffman, A., & Spezia, S. (1998). *Self-determination strategies for adolescent transitions.* Austin: Pro-Ed.

Field, S., Martin, J., Miller, R., Ward, M., Wehmeyer, M. (undated). *Self-determination for persons with disabilities: A position statement of the Division on Career Development and Transition.* Reston, VA: Council for Exceptional Children.

Flexer, R., Simmons, T., Luft, P., & Baer, R. (2001). *Transition planning for secondary students with disabilities.* Columbus, OH: Merrill Education.

Friedman, P. (2000). *Career opportunities and support services for low-income, post-high school young adults.* Welfare Information Network. Retrieved December 19, 2005 from http://www.welfareinfo.org/ issuenoteposthighschool.htm.

Furney, K., & Salembrier, G. (2000). Rhetoric and reality: A review of the literature on parent and student participation in the IEP and transition planning process. In D. R. Johnson & E. J. Emmanuel (Eds.), *Issues influencing the future of transition programs and services in the United States* (pp. 111–126). Minneapolis: University of Minnesota, Institute on Community Integration.

Gaylord, V., Johnson, D. R., Lehr, C. A., Bremer, C. D., & Hazasi, S. (Eds.). (2004). *Impact: Feature issue on achieving secondary education and transition results for students with disabilities, 16*(3). Minneapolis: University of Minnesota, Institute on Community Integration.

General Accounting Office (GAO). (2003). *Federal actions can assist state in improving postsecondary outcomes for youth* (GAO-03-773). Washington, DC: GPO.

German, S., Martin, J., Marshall, L., & Sale, H. (Spring, 2000). Promoting self-determination: Using "Take Action" to teach goal attainment. *Career Development for Exceptional Individuals, 23*(1), 27–38.

Glack, A. (2005). *What states either have, or plan to adopt, legislative or regulatory language requiring secondary transition?* Minneapolis, MN: North Central Regional Resource Center.

Glatthorn, A., & Craft-Tripp, M. (2000). *Standards-based learning for students with eisabilities.* Larchmont, NY: Eye On Education, Inc.

Gordon, H. (1999). *History and growth of vocational education in America.* Boston: Allyn and Bacon.

Grigal, M. E., Neubert, D. A., & Moon, M. S. (2005). *Transition services for students with significant disabilities in college and community setting* (Transition Series). Austin: Pro-Ed.

Greene, G., & Kochhar-Bryant, C. (2003). *Pathways to successful transition for youth with disabilities* (pp. 199–229). Columbus, OH: Merrill Prentice-Hall.

Grossi, T., Schaaf, L., Steigerwald, M., & Thomas, F. (2000). *Transition to adult life: A shared responsibility: Policy to practice guidebook.* Bloomington, IN: Center on Community Living and Careers, Indiana Institute on Disability and Community, Indiana University.

Hale, L. F. (1998). *Dropout prevention: Information and strategies for parents.* Bethesda, MD: National Association of School Psychologists.

Halloran, W., & Simon, M. (1995). The transition service requirement: A federal perspective on issues, implications and challenges. In L. West & C. Kochhar (Eds.), Emerging transition legislation for the 21st century: Special theme issue of the National Association of Vocational Special Needs Personnel. *Journal of Vocational Special Needs Education, 15*(1), 94–97.

Halpern, A. (1999). *Transition: Is it time for another rebottling?* Paper presented at the 1999 Annual OSEP Project Directors' Meeting, Washington, DC.

Halpern, A. S. (1994). The transition of youth with disabilities to adult life (pdf): A position statement of the Division on Career Development and Transition. *Career Development for Exceptional Individuals, 17*(2), 115–124.

Halpern, A. (1993). Quality of life as a conceptual framework for evaluating transition outcomes. *Exceptional Children, 59*(6).

Halpern, A. (1985). Transition: A look at the foundations. *Exceptional Children, 51,* 479–502.

Hart, D., Zafft, C., & Zimbrich, K. (Winter, 2001). Creating access to postsecondary education for all students. *The Journal for Vocational Special Needs Education, 23*(2), 19–30.

Hart, D., Zimbrich, K., & Whelley, T. (2002). *Challenges in coordinating and managing services and supports in secondary and postsecondary options.* Issue Brief, *1*(6). Minneapolis, MN: National Center for Secondary Education and Transition.

HEATH Resource Center. (2006). *The counselor toolkit.* Washington, DC: The George Washington University.

Hehir, T. (October, 1999). Begin early, end well. *The School Administrator.* Accessed 12/27/05 from http://www.aasa.org/publications/saarchive.

Hill, J. M. (1969). *The transition from school to work: A study of children's changing perception of work from the age of seven.* London: The Tavistock Institute of Human Relations.

Horne, R., & Morris, S. (March, 1999). Transition of youth with disabilities. *Liaison Bulletin, 28*(4). Alexandria, VA: National Association of State Directors of Special Education, Inc.

Individuals with Disabilities Education Act of 2004. 20 U.S.C. §1400 et seq. (2004).

Individuals with Disabilities Education Act of 1990, P.L. 101-476, 20 U.S.C. 1400. (1997).

Individuals with Disabilities Education Act Amendments of 1997, P.L. 105-17, 20 U.S.C. Chapter 33. (1997).

Izzo, M., Hertzfeld, J., Simmons-Reed, E., & Aaron, J. (2001). Promising practices: Improving the quality of higher education for students with disabilities. *Disability Studies Quarterly, 21*(1).

Jackson, T. (2003). *Secondary transition coordinators at the state level. Project Forum Brief.* Alexandria, VA: National Association of State Directors of Special Education.

Johnson, D. R., Sharpe, M. N., & Stodden, R. A. (2000). The transition to postsecondary education for students with disabilities. *Impact, 13*(1), 2–3, 26–27.

Johnson, J., & Rusch, F. (1993). Secondary special education and transition services: Identification and recommendations for future research and demonstration. *Career Development for Exceptional Individuals, 16,* 1–18.

Jorgensen, C. M. (Ed.). (1998). *Restructuring high schools for all students: Taking inclusion to the next level.* Baltimore: Paul H. Brookes.

Kavale, K. A., Holdnack, J. A,, & Mostert, M. P. (2005). Responsiveness to intervention and the identification of Specific Learning Disability: A critique and alternative proposal. *Learning Disability Quarterly, 28,* 2–16.

Kaye, H. S. (2000). Computer and internet use among people with disabilities. *Disability Statistics Report 13.* Washington, DC: U.S. Department of Education, National Institute on Disability and Rehabilitation Research.

Kochhar, C., West, L., & Taymans, J. (2000). *Successful inclusion: Practical strategies for a shared responsibility.* Englewood Cliffs, NJ: Prentice-Hall, Merrill Education Publishers.

Kochhar-Bryant, C., & Bassett, D. (2003). *Aligning transition and standards-based education.* Columbus, OH: Merrill/Prentice Hall.

Kochhar-Bryant, C. (2003). Coordinating systems and agencies for successful transition. In G. Greene & C. Kochhar-Bryant (Eds.), *Pathways to successful transition for youth with disabilities.* Columbus OH: Prentice Hall/Merrill.

Kohler, P. D. (1998). Implementing a transition perspective of education: A comprehensive approach to planning and delivering secondary education and transition services. In F. R. Rusch & J. G. Chadsey (Eds.), *Beyond high school: Transition from school to work* (pp. 179–205). New York: Wadsworth Publishing.

Kokaska, C. J., & Brolin, D. E. (1985). *Career education for handicapped individuals* (2nd ed.). New York: Merrill/Macmillan.

Kortering, L., & Braziel, P. (Fall, 2000). A look at the expressed career ambitions of youth with disabilities. *Journal for Vocational Special Needs Education 23*(1), 24–33.

Kovaleski, J., & Prasse, D. (2004). Response to instruction in the identification of learning disabilities: A guide for school teams. In A. Canter et al. (Eds.), *Helping children at home and school II: Handouts for families and educators.* Bethesda, MD: National Association of School Psychologists.

Land, D., & Legters, N. (2002). The extent and consequences of risk in U.S. education. In S. Stringfield & D. Land (Eds.), *Educating at-risk students* (pp. 1–28). Chicago: National Society for the Study of Education.

Leake, D., Kim-Rupnow, S., & Leung, P. (2003). *Issues of transition for youth with disabilities from culturally and linguistically diverse backgrounds.* Retrieved December 18, 2005 from http://ncset.org/teleconferences/ transcripts/2003_08.asp.

Leconte, P. (2006). Evolution of career, vocational, and transition assessment. In C. A. Kochhar-Bryant & M. Vreeburg Izzo (Eds.), Access to post-high school services: Transition assessment and the summary of performance. Special Issue, *Career Development for Exceptional Individuals,* Fall.

Leconte, P., & Neubert, D. A. (1997). Vocational assessment: The kick-off point for successful transitions. *Alliance: The Newsletter of the National Transition Alliance,* 2(2), 1 –4, 8.

Levine, P., Marder, C., & Wagner, M. (2004). *Services and supports for secondary school students with disabilities. A special topic report of findings from the National Longitudinal Transition Study-2* (NLTS2). Menlo Park, CA: SRI International.

Lueking, R., & Certo, N. (December, 2002). Integrating service systems at the point of transition for youth with significant disabilities: A model that works, *Addressing Trends and Developments in Secondary Education and Transition, 1*(4), 1–3. National Center for Secondary Education and Transition. Accessed 4/12/05 from www.ncset.org.

Madaus, J., Bigaj, S., Chafaleous, S., & Simonsen, B. (2006). Mining the files: What key information can be included in a comprehensive summary of performance? *Career Development for Exceptional Individuals.*

Martin, J. (2002). The transition of students with disabilities from high school to post-secondary education. In C. A. Kochhar-Bryant & D. S. Bassett (Eds.), *Aligning transition and standards-based education: Issues and strategies.* Arlington, VA: Council for Exceptional Children.

Martin, J. E., Huber Marshall, L., & Depry, R. L. (2001). Participatory decision-making. In R. Flexer, T. Simmons, P. Luft, & R. Baer (Eds.), *Transition planning for secondary students with disabilities.* Columbus, OH: Merrill Prentice-Hall.

Massachusetts Department of Education. (2005). *Transition from school to adult life.* Malden, MA.

McDonnell, L. M., McLaughlin, M. J., & Morison, P. (1997). *Educating one and all: Students with disabilities and standards-based reform.* National Research Council. Washington, DC: National Academy Press.

McNeil, J. M. (2000). *Employment, earnings, and disability.* Prepared for the 75th Annual Conference of the Western Economic Association International, June 29–July 3.

Michaels, C. A. (1994). *Transition strategies for persons with learning disabilities.* San Diego, CA: Singular.

National Center on Education, Disability and Juvenile Justice. (2004). *Transition planning and services.* College Park: University of Maryland.

National Center for Education Statistics (NCES). (June, 1999). *Students with disabilities in postsecondary education: A profile of preparation, participation, and outcomes.* Washington, DC: Author.

National Center for Secondary Education and Transition (NCSET). (November 17, 2004). Preparing for post-secondary education. *NCSET Topics.* Minneapolis, MN: NCSET.

National Center for Secondary Education and Transition (NCSET). (2002). Integrating services systems at the point of transition for youth with significant disabilities: A model that works. *NCSET Information Brief, 1*(4). Minneapolis, MN: NCSET.

112

National Center for the Study of Postsecondary Educational Supports. (2002). *Preparation for and support of youth with disabilities in postsecondary education and employment: Implications for policy, priorities and practice.* Proceedings and briefing book for the National Summit on Postsecondary Education for People with Disabilities, Washington, DC, July 8, 2002, p. 11.

National Council on Disability. (2000). *Transition and post-school outcomes for youth with disabilities: Closing the gaps to post-secondary education and employment.* Washington, DC.

National Council for Research on Women. (2001). *Balancing the equation: Where are women and girls in science, engineering and technology?* New York: Author.

National Council for Research on Women. (1998). *Girls report.* New York: Author.

National Information Center for Children and Youth with Disabilities (NICH-CY). (2002). *Transition planning: A team effort.* Transition Summary 10 (TS10) 1999. Washington, DC: Author.

National Joint Committee on Learning Disabilities. (2005). *Responsiveness to intervention and learning disabilities.* Retrieved on September 1, 2005 from http://www.TeachingLD.org/pdf/rti_final.pdf.htm.

National Council on Disability. (September 15, 2003). *People with disabilities and post-secondary education.* Position Paper. Washington, DC: National Council on Disability.

National Organization on Disability/Louis Harris & Associates, Inc. (2000). *Harris survey of Americans with disabilities.* New York: Author.

Neubert, D. (2003). The role of assessment in the transition to adult life process for students with disabilities. *Exceptionality, 11*(2), 63–75.

Neubert, D. A. (2000). Transition education and services guidelines. In G. M. Clark, P. Sitlington, & O. P. Kolstoe (Eds.). *Transition education and services for adolescents with disabilities* (3rd ed.), pp. 39–69. Boston: Allyn and Bacon.

New York State Department of Education. (2005). *Sample Individualized Education Program (IEP) and guidance document.* Albany: The University of the State of New York and the State Education Department, Office of Vocational and Educational Services.

No Child Left Behind Act of 2001, P.L. 107-110, 20 U.S.C. §6301 et seq.

O'Leary, E., & Collision, W. (2002). *Transition services: Helping educators, parents and other stakeholders understand.* Mountain Plains Regional Resource Center. Accessed 12/28/05 from http://www1.usu.edu/mprrc/curproj/sectrans/materials/transitionservices.cfm#2.

Patton, J. R., & Blalock, G. (1996). *Transition and students with disabilities.* Austin, TX: Pro-Ed.

Patton, J. R. & Dunn, C. (1998). *Transition from school to young adulthood: Basic concepts and recommended practices.* Austin, TX: Pro-Ed.

Patton, J., & Trainor, A. (2003). Utilizing applied academics to enhance curricular reform in secondary education. In C. A. Kochhar-Bryant & D. S. Bassett (Eds.), *Aligning transition and standards-based education: Issues and strategies.* Arlington, VA: Council for Exceptional Children.

Polloway, E., Patton, J., Smith, J., & Rodrique, T. (1991). Issues in program design for elementary students with mental retardation: Emphasis on curriculum development. *Education and Training in Mental Retardation, 26,* 142–250.

President's Commission on Excellence in Special Education. (2002). *A new era: Revitalizing special education for children and their families.* Jessup, MD: Educational Publications.

Repetto, J., Webb, K., Neubert, D. A., & Curran, C. (2006). *Succeeding with middle school learners: Using universal design to promote transition and self-determination.* Austin, TX: Pro-Ed.

Rehabilitation Act Amendments of 1998, Section 504 (29 USC Section 794), P.L. 102-569.

Research and Training Center on Service Coordination. (2001). *Data report: Service coordination policies and models.* Research and Training Center on Service Coordination: Division of Child and Family Studies. Storrs: University of Connecticut Health Center.

Rothenbacher, C., & Leconte, P. (1990). Transition services in the IEP. *NICHCY Transition Summary, 3*(1). #TS8, March, 1993, National Information Center for Children and Youth with Disabilities (NICHCY). Washington, DC.

Rutherford, R. B., Jr., & Quinn, M. M. (November/December, 1999). Special education in alternative education programs. *The Clearing House, 73*(2), 79–81.

Scharff, D., & Hill, J. (1976). *Between two worlds: Aspects of transition from school to work.* London: Consultant Books.

Schiller, E., Burnaska, K., Cohen, G., Douglas, Z., Joseph, C., Johnston, P., et al. (2003). *Study of state and local implementation and impact of the Individuals with Disabilities Education Act—Final report on selected findings.* Bethesda, MD: Abt Associates Inc.

Scott, S., Shaw, S., & McGuire, J. (in press). Universal Design for Instruction: A new paradigm for adult instruction in postsecondary education. *Remedial and Special Education.*

Shafer, M. S., & Rangasamy, R. (1995). Transition for youth with learning disabilities: A focus on developing independence. *Learning Disabilities Quarterly, 15,* 237–249.

Shaw, S. F. (2005). IDEA will change the face of postsecondary disability documentation. *Disability Compliance for Higher Education, 11*(1), 7.

Shaw, S. F., & Dukes, L. L. (2001). Program standards for disability services in higher education. *Journal of Postsecondary Education and Disability, 14*(2), 81–90.

Shaw, S., Kochhar-Bryant, C., Izzo, M., Benedict, K., & Parker, D. (2005). *Summary of Performance under IDEA 2004.* National Documentation Summit.

Sitlington, P., & Clark, G. (2006). *Transition education and services for students with disabilities.* Boston: Allyn and Bacon.

Sitlington, P. L., & Neubert, D. A. (1998). Assessment for life: Methods and processes to determine students' interests, abilities, and preferences. In M. Wehmeyer & D. J. Sands (Eds.), *Making it happen: Student involvement in educational planning, decision making, and instruction* (pp. 75–98). Baltimore: Paul H. Brookes.

Smith, F., & Leconte, P. (2004). Universal design for learning: Assuring access and success for all. *VSTE Journal 19*(1), 25–29. Retrieved December 27, 2004 from http://www.vste.org/communication/journal.

Social Security Administration Annual Statistics. (2001). *Annual statistical report on the Social Security Disability Insurance Program, 2000.* Washington, DC: Social Security Administration, Office of Policy.

Stodden, R., & Welley , M. (2002). *Post-secondary supports for individuals with disabilities: Latest research findings.* Manoa: National Center for the Study of Postsecondary Educational Supports, Center on Disability Studies, University of Hawaii at Manoa.

Storms, J., O'Leary, E., & Williams, J. (2000). *The Individuals with Disabilities Education Act of 1997 transition requirements: A guide for states, districts, schools, universities and families.* National Transition Network Institute on Community Integration (UAP). Minneapolis: University of Minnesota.

Study of Personnel Needs in Special Education. (2002). *General education teacher's role in special education.* Gainesville: University of Florida.

Tashie, C., Shapiro-Barnard, S., Dillon, A., Schuh, M., & Jorgenson, C. (2001). *Changes in latitudes, changes in attitudes: The role of the inclusion facilitator.* Nottingham, UK: Inclusive Solutions.

Thompson, J. R., Fulk, B. M., & Piercy, S. W. (2000). Do individualized transition plans match the postschool projections of students and parents? *Career Development for Exceptional Individuals, 23,* 3–26.

U.S. Congress. (1997). United States House Committee report on IDEA amendments, H.R. No. 105-95, p. 102.

U.S. Department of Education. (March 2, 2004a). *Letter to chief state school officers regarding inclusion of students with disabilities in state accountability systems.* Washington, DC: Author.

U.S. Department of Education. (2004b). *SLIIDEA study.* Washington, DC: GPO.

U.S. Department of Education. (2003). *Twenty Fifth Annual Report to Congress on the implementation of IDEA.* Washington, DC: GPO.

U.S. Department of Education. (2002). *Students with disabilities preparing for postsecondary education: Know your rights and responsibilities.* Washington, DC: Office for Civil Rights.

U.S. Department of Education. (2001). *Twenty-Third Annual Report to Congress on the Implementation of IDEA.* Washington, DC: GPO.

U.S. Department of Education. (1992, September 29). Assistance to states for the Education of Children with Disabilities Program and Preschool Grants for Children with Disabilities; Final rules. *Federal Register, 57*(208), 48644–48704.

U.S. Department of Health, Education, and Welfare. (1977). *Federal policy on education and work.* Washington, DC: GPO.

U.S. Department of Justice, Office of Civil Rights. (2002). *Students with disabilities preparing for postsecondary education: Know your rights and responsibilities.* Washington, DC: U.S. Department of Education.

U.S. Office of Civil Rights. (2002). *Students with disabilities preparing for postsecondary education: Know your rights and responsibilities.* Washington, DC: U.S. Department of Education.

U.S. Office of Special Education. (1994). *National agenda for achieving better results for children and youth with disabilities.* U.S. Department of Education. Washington, DC: The Cosmos Corporation.

Virginia Department of Education. (2004). *Virginia Transition Outcomes Project.* Richmond, VA: Author.

Vocational Education Act (P.L. 88-210).

Wagner, M., Newman, L., Cameto, R., & Levine, P. (2005). *National longitudinal transition study 2: Changes over time in the early post-school outcomes of youth with disabilities.* Menlo Park, CA: SRI International.

Wandry, D., & Repetto, J. (March, 1993). Transition services in the IEP. *NICHCY Transition Summary, 3*(1), #TS8.

Ward, M., & Halloran, W. (1993). *OSERS News in Print: Transitions, 6*(1). U.S. Department of Education, Office of Special Education Programs.

Wehman, P. (2001). *Life beyond the classroom: Transition strategies for young people with disabilities* (3rd ed.). Baltimore: Paul H. Brookes.

Wehmeyer, M. (2003). Transition principles and access to the general education curriculum. In C. A. Kochhar-Bryant & D. S. Bassett (Eds.), *Aligning transition and standards-based education: Issues and strategies.* Arlington, VA: Council for Exceptional Children.

Wehman, P. H., Kregel, J., Barcus, J. M., & Schalock, R. L. (1986). Vocational transition for students with developmental disabilities. In W. E. Kiernan & L. Stark (Eds.), *Pathways to employment for adults with developmental disabilities* (pp. 113–127). Baltimore: Paul H. Brookes.

Weidenthal, C., & Kochhar-Bryant, C. A. (in press). *Transition practices for young adolescents: Implications for policy and practice.*

Will, M. (1985). Educating children with learning problems: A shared responsibility. *Exceptional Children, 52*(5), 411–415.

Youth Employment and Demonstration Projects Act of 1977 (P.L. 95-93).

Ysseldyke, J., Olsen, K., & Thurlow, M. (1997). *NCEO synthesis report 27: Issues and considerations in alternate assessments.* Minneapolis: University of Minnesota, National Center on Educational Outcomes.

Ysseldyke, J. E., Thurlow, M. L., Langenfeld, K. L., Nelson, J. R., Teelucksing, E., & Seyfurth, A. (1998). *Educational results for students with disabilities: What do the data tell us?* (Technical Report No. 23). Minneapolis: University of Minnesota, National Center on Educational Outcomes.

Index

117

119